Winnie-the-Pooh

by A. A. Milne
With decorations by E. H. Shepard

Level 3
(1600-word)

Retold by Ikhlas Abdul Hadi

IBC パブリッシング

はじめに

　ラダーシリーズは、「はしご (ladder)」を使って一歩一歩上を目指すように、学習者の実力に合わせ、無理なくステップアップできるよう開発された英文リーダーのシリーズです。

　リーディング力をつけるためには、繰り返したくさん読むこと、いわゆる「多読」がもっとも効果的な学習法であると言われています。多読では、「1. 速く　2. 訳さず英語のまま　3. なるべく辞書を使わず」に読むことが大切です。スピードを計るなど、速く読むよう心がけましょう（たとえば TOEIC® テストの音声スピードはおよそ 1 分間に 150 語です）。そして一語ずつ訳すのではなく、英語を英語のまま理解するくせをつけるようにします。こうして読み続けるうちに語感がついてきて、だんだんと英語が理解できるようになるのです。まずは、ラダーシリーズの中からあなたのレベルに合った本を選び、少しずつ英文に慣れ親しんでください。たくさんの本を手にとるうちに、英文書がすらすら読めるようになってくるはずです。

《本シリーズの特徴》

- 中学校レベルから中級者レベルまで5段階に分かれています。自分に合ったレベルからスタートしてください。
- クラシックから現代文学、ノンフィクション、ビジネスと幅広いジャンルを扱っています。あなたの興味に合わせてタイトルを選べます。
- 巻末のワードリストで、いつでもどこでも単語の意味を確認できます。レベル1、2では、文中の全ての単語が、レベル3以上は中学校レベル外の単語が掲載されています。
- カバーにヘッドホーンマークのついているタイトルは、オーディオ・サポートがあります。ウェブから購入／ダウンロードし、リスニング教材としても併用できます。

《使用語彙について》

レベル1：中学校で学習する単語約1000語

レベル2：レベル1の単語＋使用頻度の高い単語約300語

レベル3：レベル1の単語＋使用頻度の高い単語約600語

レベル4：レベル1の単語＋使用頻度の高い単語約1000語

レベル5：語彙制限なし

Winnie-the-Pooh

CONTENTS

Chapter 1

In which we are introduced to Winnie-the-Pooh
and some Bees, and the stories begin   9

Chapter 2

In which Pooh goes visiting and
gets into a tight place   25

Chapter 3

In which Pooh and Piglet go hunting
and nearly catch a Woozle   36

Chapter 4

In which Eeyore loses a tail
and Pooh finds one   45

Chapter 5

In which Piglet meets a Heffalump   55

Chapter 6

In which Eeyore has a birthday
and gets two presents   69

Chapter 7

In which Kanga and Baby Roo come to the Forest,
and Piglet has a bath   85

Chapter 8

In which Christopher Robin leads an expotition
to the North Pole   102

Chapter 9

In which Piglet is entirely surrounded by water   120

Chapter 10

In which Christopher Robin gives a Pooh Party,
and we say good-bye   135

Word List   150

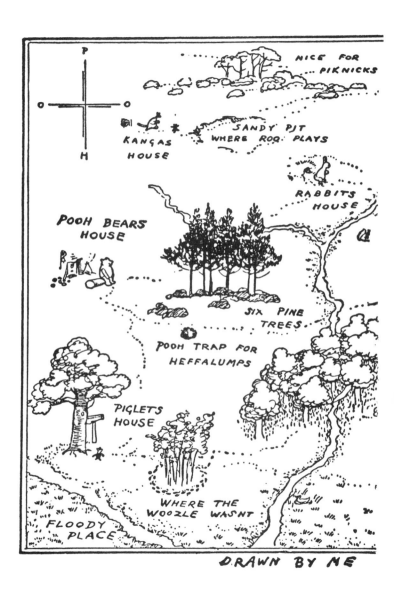

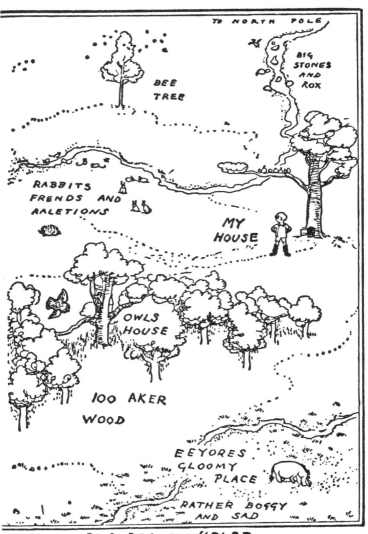

読みはじめる前に

この本で使われている用語です。わからない語は巻末のワードリストで確認しましょう。

- [ ] bother
- [ ] branch
- [ ] bump
- [ ] bush
- [ ] buzz
- [ ] expedition
- [ ] fierce
- [ ] gloomily
- [ ] jar
- [ ] North Pole
- [ ] paw
- [ ] silly
- [ ] squeak
- [ ] stump
- [ ] tail
- [ ] trespasser
- [ ] trick
- [ ] whisper

登場キャラクター

Winnie the Pooh ウィニー・ザ・プー　食いしん坊で頭のよくないクマ

Christopher Robin クリストファー・ロビン　人間の男の子

Piglet ピグレット　プーの親友で、こわがりの子豚

Rabbit ラビット　ちょっと神経質なウサギ

Kanga and Roo カンガとルー　カンガルーの親子

Eeyore イーヨー　陰気なロバ

Owl オウル　物知り顔のフクロウ

Heffalump ヘッファランプ　ゾウに似た空想上の動物

Wizzle, Woozle ウィズル、ウーズル　イタチに似た空想上の動物

To Her

Hand in hand we come
    Christopher Robin and I
To lay this book in your lap.
        Say you're surprised?
        Say you like it?
        Say it's just what you wanted?
            Because it's yours—
            Because we love you.

CHAPTER ONE

In which we are introduced to Winnie-the-Pooh and some Bees, and the stories begin

Here is Edward Bear coming down the stairs. Bump, bump, bump. He thinks it is the only way to go downstairs. Sometimes he thinks there is another way. Then he thinks maybe there isn't. And here he is with Christopher Robin, ready to be introduced. Winnie-the-Pooh.

When I heard his name, I said, "I thought he was a boy?"

"So did I," said Christopher Robin.

"You don't call him Winnie?"

"I don't."

"But you said—"

"He's Winnie-ther-Pooh. Don't you know what '*ther*' means?"

"Ah, yes, now I do," I said quickly.

Sometimes Winnie-the-Pooh wants a game

when he comes downstairs. Sometimes he wants a story. This evening—

"Could you tell Winnie-the-Pooh a story, please?"
"Maybe," I said. "What type of stories does he like?"
"He likes stories about himself."
"Oh, I see."
"So could you, please?"
"I'll try," I said.
So I tried.

* * *

We are Introduced

Once upon a time, Winnie-the-Pooh lived in a forest under the name of Sanders.

(*"What does 'under the name' mean?" asked Christopher Robin.*

"It means the name 'Sanders' is hung over the door and he lived under it."

"Winnie-the-Pooh wasn't sure," said Christopher Robin.

"Now I am," said a growly voice.

"Then I will continue," said I.)

One day he was out walking, and he found a place in the middle of the forest. In the middle of this place was a large oak tree. On top of that tree was a loud buzzing-noise.

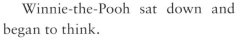

Winnie-the-Pooh sat down and began to think.

First he said: "That buzzing-noise means somebody is making a buzzing-noise. And you make a buzzing-noise if you are a bee."

He thought for a long time, and said: "Bees make honey."

Then he got up, and said: "And bees make honey so *I* can eat it." So he began to climb the tree.

He
climbed
and
he
climbed
and
he
climbed.
As
he
climbed
he
sang
a
song:

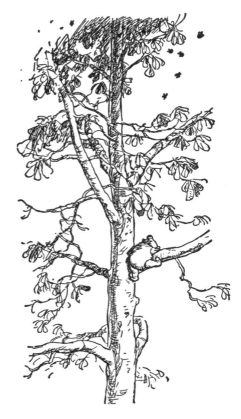

Isn't it funny
How a bear likes honey?
Buzz! Buzz! Buzz!
I wonder why he does?

He climbed higher . . . and higher . . . and then higher. By that time he had a new song.

It's funny to think that if Bears were Bees,
They would build their nests at the *bottom* of
    trees.
If that is true (if Bees were Bears),
We would not have to climb up all these stairs.

He was almost there now. If he stood on that branch . . .
Crack!
"Oh, help!" said Pooh as he fell to the branch below.
"If only—" he said, as he fell to the next branch.

"What I *wanted* to do," he explained, as he crashed to another branch below.

"It is all because," he decided, as he landed in a bush, "it is all because I *like* honey so much. Oh, help!"

He crawled out of the bush and he began to think again. The first person he thought about was Christopher Robin.

(*"Was that me?" said a surprised Christopher Robin.*

"That was you."

Christopher Robin said nothing, but his eyes grew large, and his face turned pink.)

So Winnie-the-Pooh visited his friend Christopher Robin. His friend lived behind a green door in another part of the Forest.

"Good morning, Christopher Robin," he said.
"Good morning, Winnie-*ther*-Pooh," said you.
"I was wondering if you had a balloon?"
"A balloon?"
"Yes."
"Why do you want a balloon?" you said.
Winnie-the-Pooh checked that nobody was listening. He put his paw to his mouth, and said in a whisper: "*Honey!*"
"But you don't get honey with balloons!"

"*I* do," said Pooh.

Well, yesterday you went to a party at Piglet's house and there were balloons at the party. You had a big green balloon. One of Rabbit's family members had a big blue balloon, but left it behind. So you brought home the green *and* the blue balloons.

"Which one would you like?" you asked Pooh.

He put his head between his paws and thought carefully.

"Well," he said. "When you go after honey, you must not let the bees know you're coming. With a green balloon, the bees might think you were part of the tree.

"With a blue balloon, they might think you were part of the sky. But which is better?"

"Wouldn't they see *you* with the balloon?" you asked.

"They might or they might not," said Winnie-the-Pooh. "You never know with bees." He thought for a moment and said: "I will try to look like a small black cloud. That will trick them."

"Then you should take the blue balloon," you said.

You both left the house with the blue balloon. You also took your gun, like always. Winnie-the-Pooh went to a muddy place. He rolled and rolled until he was black all over. The balloon was blown up very big and you and Pooh held on to the string.

And then you let go. Pooh Bear floated up into the sky, and stayed there. But he was too far from the tree.

"Hooray!" you shouted.

"What do I look like?" shouted Winnie-the-Pooh.

"You look like a Bear holding on to a balloon," you said.

"Not like a small black cloud in a blue sky?" said Pooh anxiously.

"No."

"Maybe it looks different from up here. You never know with bees."

There was no wind to blow him closer to the tree. He could see the honey, he could smell the honey, but he couldn't reach the honey.

After a while he called in a loud whisper.

"Christopher Robin!"

"Yes!"

"I think the bees *suspect* something!"

"What do they suspect?"

WE ARE INTRODUCED

"I don't know. But I think they're *suspicious*!"

"Maybe they think you're after their honey?"

"Maybe. You never know with bees."

There was another silence. And then he called down again.

"Christopher Robin!"

"Yes?"

"Do you have an umbrella in your house?"

"I think so."

"Could you bring your umbrella and walk around with it? Then look up at me and say, 'Tut-tut, it looks like rain.' I think if you did that, it would help trick these bees."

You laughed to yourself, "Silly old Bear!" But you didn't say it out loud because you loved him, and you went home for your umbrella.

"Oh, there you are!" called Winnie-the-Pooh, when you got back to the tree. "I was getting anxious. These bees are definitely Suspicious."

"Shall I open my umbrella?" you said.

"Yes, but the important bee to trick is the Queen Bee. Can you see the Queen Bee from down there?"

"No."

"Too bad. Then can you walk around with your umbrella, saying 'Tut-tut, it looks like rain'? I will sing a Cloud Song... Go!"

So, you walked around and wondered if it would rain. Winnie-the-Pooh sang:

How sweet to be a Cloud
    Floating in the Blue!
Every little cloud
Always sings out loud.

"How sweet to be a Cloud
    Floating in the Blue!"
It makes him very proud
To be a little cloud.

The bees buzzed even more suspiciously.

"Christopher—*ow!*—Robin," called the cloud.

"Yes?"

"*These are the wrong type of bees.*"

"Are they?"

"Yes. And I think they make the wrong type of honey."

"Do they?"

"Yes. So I will come down."

"How?" asked you.

Winnie-the-Pooh had not thought about this. If he let go of the string, he would fall—*bump*—and he didn't like that. So he thought for a long time. Then he said:

"Christopher Robin, you must shoot the balloon with your gun."

"But if I do that, it will break the balloon," you said.

"But if you *don't*," said Pooh, "I have to let go, and that would break me."

So you pointed your gun at the balloon carefully, and shot.

"*Ow!*" said Pooh.

"Did I miss?" you asked.

"You missed *the balloon*," said Pooh.

"I'm so sorry," you said. You shot again, and this time you hit the balloon. The air came out, and Winnie-the-Pooh floated down.

His arms were stiff from holding the balloon for so long. They stayed up for over a week. Whenever a fly sat on his nose he had to blow it off.

We are Introduced

And I think *that* is why he was called Pooh.

* * *

"Is that the end?" asked Christopher Robin.

"That's the end of this story. There are other stories."

"About Pooh and Me?"

"And Piglet and Rabbit and all of you. Do you remember?"

"I remember, but sometimes I forget."

"That day when Pooh and Piglet tried to catch the Heffalump—"

"They didn't catch it, right?"

"No."

"Did *I* catch it?"

"Well, that's part of the story."

Christopher Robin nodded.

"I remember," he said, "but Pooh doesn't. That's why he likes listening to the stories. Because then they become real."

"That's just how *I* feel," I said.

Christopher Robin sighed deeply, picked his bear up by the leg and walked toward the door. Then he turned and said, "Coming to see me have my bath?"

"Maybe," I said.

"Did I hurt him when I shot him?"

"Not at all."

He nodded and went out... and in a moment I heard Winnie-the-Pooh—*bump, bump, bump*—going up the stairs behind him.

CHAPTER TWO

In which Pooh goes visiting and gets into a tight place

One day, Edward Bear (or Winnie-the-Pooh, or Pooh for short) was taking a walk and humming to himself. He had made up a little hum that morning when he was doing his Stoutness Exercises: *Tra-la-la, tra-la-la*, as he stretched up high. Then *Tra-la-la, tra-la—oh, help!—la*, as he tried to reach his toes. He repeated the hum until he knew it by heart. Now he hummed it properly. It went:

Tra-la-la, tra-la-la,
Rum-tum-tiddle-um-tum.
Tiddle-iddle, tiddle-iddle,
Rum-tum-tum-tiddle-um.

He was happily humming this to himself

Winnie-the-Pooh

while walking. Suddenly, he came to a large hole.

"Aha!" said Pooh. (*Rum-tum-tiddle-um-tum*.) "That hole means Rabbit," he said, "and Rabbit means Company," he said, "and Company means Food and Listening-to-Me-Humming. *Rum-tum-tum-tiddle-um*."

So he put his head into the hole, and called out:

"Is anybody home?"

A noise came from inside the hole, and then silence.

"I said, 'Anybody home?'" called out Pooh loudly.

"No!" said a voice; and then, "Don't shout. I heard you the first time."

"Bother!" said Pooh. "Is there nobody here?"

"Nobody."

Winnie-the-Pooh thought to himself, "There must be somebody there. Somebody must have *said* 'Nobody.'"

So he said:

"Hallo, Rabbit, is that you?"

"No," said Rabbit, in a different voice.

"But isn't that Rabbit's voice?"

"I don't *think* so," said Rabbit. "It isn't *meant* to be."

"Oh!" said Pooh. "Well, could you please tell me where Rabbit is?"

"He went to see his friend Pooh Bear."

"But that is Me!" said Bear, surprised.

"What sort of Me?"

"Pooh Bear."

"Are you sure?" said Rabbit.

"Very sure," said Pooh.

"Then, come in."

So Pooh pushed and pushed and pushed his way through the hole, and got in.

POOH GOES VISITING

"It *is* you," said Rabbit. "Glad to see you."

"Who did you think it was?"

"I wasn't sure. But I had to be *careful* living here in the forest. Do you want to eat something?"

Pooh always liked to have something to eat, so he was glad when Rabbit took out the plates and mugs. When Rabbit said, "Honey or condensed milk with your bread?" Pooh became excited. He said, "Both, but I don't need the bread." And then he ate silently for a long time...until finally, he got up. He shook Rabbit's paw lovingly, and said that he must leave.

"Must you?" said Rabbit politely.

"Well," said Pooh, "I could stay longer if you—" He looked around for more food.

"Actually," said Rabbit, "I was also leaving."

"Oh, then, I will also leave. Good-bye."

"Well, good-bye, if you won't have any more."

"*Is* there any more?" asked Pooh quickly.

Rabbit showed the dishes, and said, "No, there isn't."

29

"I thought so," said Pooh, nodding. "Well, good-bye, I must leave."

So he began climbing out of the hole. He pushed and pulled, and soon his nose was out in the open again...and then his ears...and then his front paws...and then his shoulders...and then—

"Oh, help, I'm stuck!" said Pooh. "Oh, help *and* bother!"

Now, by this time Rabbit wanted to go for a walk too. He saw that the front door was full, so he went out the back door. Outside, he met Pooh.

"Hallo, are you stuck?" he asked.

"N-no," said Pooh. "Just resting and thinking and humming to myself."

"Here, give me your paw."

Pooh Bear gave his paw. Rabbit pulled and pulled and pulled...

"*Ow!*" cried Pooh. "It hurts!"

"You're stuck," said Rabbit.

"It's because," said Pooh crossly, "your front doors aren't big enough."

"It's because you ate too much," said Rabbit sternly. "Well, I shall go and fetch Christopher Robin."

Christopher Robin came with Rabbit. When he saw the front half of Pooh, he said, "Silly old Bear," in a loving voice. Everybody felt hopeful again.

"I was just thinking," said Bear, sniffing, "that Rabbit might never use his front door again."

"Of course he'll use his front door again." said Christopher Robin.

"Good," said Rabbit.

"If we can't pull you out, Pooh, we could push you in."

Rabbit scratched his whiskers thoughtfully. He said that if Pooh was pushed inside, he might stay inside forever and—

"You mean I'd *never* get out?" said Pooh.

"I mean," said Rabbit, "you're already *so* far out, we shouldn't push you in again."

Christopher Robin nodded.

"There's only one thing to do," he said. "We have to wait for you to get thin again."

"How long does that take?" asked Pooh anxiously.

"About a week."

Pooh Goes Visiting

"But I can't stay here for a *week*!"

"You can definitely *stay* here, silly old Bear. Getting you out is the difficult part."

"We'll read to you," said Rabbit cheerfully.

"And I hope you *don't* mind," he added. "if I use your back legs as a towel-rack? They aren't doing anything and it would be good to hang towels on them."

"A week!" said Pooh gloomily. "*What about food?*"

"No food," said Christopher Robin, "because you need to get thinner. But we *will* read to you."

A tear rolled down his eye, and Bear said:

"Would you read me a Sustaining Book? It would make me very happy."

So for a week Christopher Robin read that type of book to Pooh's head.

33

And Rabbit hung his towels on Pooh's legs... and Bear felt himself get thinner and thinner. At the end of the week Christopher Robin said, "*Now!*"

Pooh Goes Visiting

He held Pooh's front paws and Rabbit held Christopher Robin, and Rabbit's friends and family held Rabbit. And they all pulled...

Pooh said "*Ow!*"...

And "*Oh!*"...

And then, he said "*Pop!*"

And Christopher Robin and Rabbit and Rabbit's friends and family all fell over backwards... and then came Winnie-the-Pooh—free!

He thanked his friends, and went on with his walk. He hummed proudly to himself. Christopher Robin watched him lovingly. He said, "Silly old Bear!"

CHAPTER THREE

In which Pooh and Piglet go hunting and nearly catch a Woozle

Piglet lived in the middle of a grand house in the middle of a beech-tree in the forest. Next to his house was a broken board which read: "TRESPASSERS W." When Christopher Robin asked what it meant, Piglet said it was his grandfather's name. Christopher Robin said you *couldn't* be called Trespassers W. Piglet said yes, you could, because his grandfather's name was Trespassers Will, short for Trespassers William. Piglet's grandfather had two names in case he lost one.

"I have two names," said Christopher Robin.

"Well, there you go," said Piglet.

One winter's day, Piglet was brushing away the snow in front of his house. He looked up, and saw Winnie-the-Pooh. Pooh was walking

around in a circle.

Piglet called to him, but Pooh just continued walking.

"Hallo!" said Piglet, "what are *you* doing?"

"Tracking something," said Winnie-the-Pooh mysteriously.

"Tracking what?" said Piglet, coming closer.

"I will know once I find it," said Winnie-the-Pooh. "Look." He pointed to the ground.

"What do you see?"

"Tracks," said Piglet. "Paw-marks." He squeaked excitedly. "Oh, Pooh! Do you think it's a—a—a Woozle?"

"Maybe," said Pooh. "Sometimes it is, and sometimes it isn't. You can never tell with paw-marks."

Then he went on tracking. Piglet watched him for a few minutes, then ran after him. Winnie-the-Pooh stopped suddenly. He bent over the tracks, puzzled.

"What's the matter?" asked Piglet.

"It's funny," said Bear, "but there are *two* animals now. This—whatever-it-was—has been joined by another—whatever-it-is—and the two of them are walking together. Would you mind coming with me, Piglet, in case they are Hostile Animals?"

Pooh and Piglet Hunt

Piglet said that he would be happy to come, in case it really *was* a Woozle.

"You mean, in case it really is two Woozles," said Winnie-the-Pooh. So off they went together.

It seemed that the two Woozles, if that is what they were, had been going around an area of larch-trees. So Pooh and Piglet went around

this area after them. As they walked, Piglet told Pooh about Grandfather Trespassers W and how he Removed Stiffness after Tracking, and how Grandfather Trespassers W had a Shortness of Breath when he was older. Pooh wondered what a Grandfather was like and he wondered whether maybe they were tracking Two Grandfathers instead of two Woozles. If so, he wondered if he could take one Grandfather home and keep it.

Suddenly Winnie-the-Pooh stopped, and pointed excitedly. "*Look!*"

"*What?*" said Piglet with a jump.

"The tracks!" said Pooh. "*A third animal has joined them!*"

"Pooh!" cried Piglet. "Do you think it is another Woozle?"

"No," said Pooh, "the marks are different. It is either Two Woozles and one Wizzle, or Two Wizzles and one Woozle. Let us continue to follow them."

So they continued, a little anxious now. The three unknown animals could have Hostile Intent. Piglet wished that his Grandfather T. W. were there. Pooh thought it would be nice if they met Christopher Robin accidentally, because he liked Christopher Robin so much. Suddenly, Winnie-the-Pooh stopped and licked the tip of his nose to cool himself. He was feeling hot and anxious. *There were four animals in front of them!*

"Look at the tracks! Three Woozles, and one Wizzle. *Another Woozle has joined them!*"

And so it seemed to be. The tracks were crossed and muddled together. But, it was clear that there were four sets of paws.

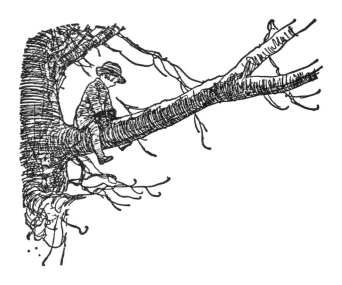

"I *think*," said Piglet, licking the tip of his nose, but not finding it comforting, "I *think* that I just remembered something. I forgot to do something yesterday that I can't do tomorrow. So I should go and do it now."

"We'll do it this afternoon. I'll come with you," said Pooh.

"You can't do it in the afternoon," said Piglet quickly. "It has to be done in the morning, and, if possible, at—What time is it?"

"About twelve," said Winnie-the-Pooh, looking at the sun.

"At, as I was saying, twelve. So, dear old Pooh, if you'll excuse me—*What's that?*"

Pooh looked up into the branches of a big oak tree.

"It's Christopher Robin," he said.

"Ah, then you'll be quite safe with *him*," said Piglet.

"Good-bye now," and he went home quickly, glad to be Out of Danger.

Christopher Robin came slowly down his tree.

"Silly old Bear," he said, "what *were* you doing? You went around the area twice by yourself. Then you and Piglet went around again together. And then you were just going around a fourth time—"

"Wait a minute," said Winnie-the-Pooh, holding up his paw.

He sat down to think. He fitted his paw into a Track . . . then he scratched his nose, and stood up.

"I see now," said Winnie-the-Pooh.

"I have been Foolish," said he, "and I am a Bear of No Brain."

"You're the Best Bear in the World," said Christopher Robin.

"Am I?" said Pooh hopefully. And then he brightened up.

"Anyhow," he said, "it is nearly Luncheon Time."

So he went home for lunch.

CHAPTER FOUR

In which Eeyore loses a tail and Pooh finds one

The Old Grey Donkey, Eeyore, stood alone in the Forest. He was thinking. Sometimes he thought sadly to himself, "Why?" and sometimes he thought, "Wherefore?"—and sometimes he didn't know what he *was* thinking about. So when Winnie-the-Pooh appeared, Eeyore was happy to stop thinking for a while. He said gloomily "How do you do?"

"And how are you?" said Winnie-the-Pooh.

"Not very how," Eeyore said, shaking his head. "I haven't felt how for a long time."

"Dear, dear," said Pooh, "I'm sorry about that. Let's take a look at you."

So Eeyore gazed sadly at the ground, and Winnie-the-Pooh walked around him.

"What's happened to your tail?" he said, surprised.

"What *has* happened to it?" said Eeyore.

"It isn't there!"

"Are you sure?"

"Well, either a tail is there or it isn't there. And yours *isn't* there!"

"Let's have a look," said Eeyore. He turned slowly to see his tail. When he couldn't see it, he turned the other way. Still unable to see it, he put his head down and looked between his front legs. At last he said, with a sad sigh, "I believe you're right."

"Of course," said Pooh.

"That Explains Everything," said Eeyore gloomily.

"Somebody must have taken it," said Eeyore. "How Like Them," he added, after a long silence.

Pooh wanted to say something helpful, but didn't know what. So he decided to do something helpful instead.

"Eeyore," he said, "I, Winnie-the-Pooh, will find your tail for you."

"Thank you, Pooh," answered Eeyore. "You're a real friend."

So Winnie-the-Pooh went to find Eeyore's tail.

It was a fine spring morning in the Forest.

There were little clouds playing in a blue sky, and the sun was shining. Bear marched through the trees; down slopes of heather, over streams, then up and into the heather again. At last, tired and hungry, he arrived at the Hundred Acre Wood. It was where Owl lived.

"If anyone knows anything about anything, it's Owl," said Bear, "or my name's not Winnie-the-Pooh," he said. "Which it is," he added. "So there you are."

Owl lived at The Chestnuts, a charming old home. Bear thought it was a grand house because it had a knocker *and* a bell-rope.

Under the knocker, a sign read:

PLES RING IF AN RNSER IS REQIRD.

Under the bell-rope, a sign read:

PLEZ CNOKE IF AN RNSR IS NOT REQID.

These signs were written by Christopher Robin, the only person in the forest who could spell. Even wise Owl could not spell. He could only read and write.

Eeyore Loses a Tail

Winnie-the-Pooh read the two signs very carefully. Then, to be quite sure, he knocked and pulled the knocker, and he pulled and knocked the bell-rope. He called loudly, "Owl! It's Bear speaking." The door opened, and Owl looked out.

"Hallo, Pooh," he said. "How's things?"

"Terrible," said Pooh, "because Eeyore, my friend, has lost his tail. And now he's Sad. Could you kindly help me find it for him?"

"Well," said Owl, "the customary procedure is as follows."

"What is Crustimoney Proseedcake?" said Pooh. "I am a Bear of Very Little Brain, and long words Bother me."

"It means the Thing to Do."

"If it means that, that's fine," said Pooh.

"The thing to do is as follows. First, Issue a Reward. Then—"

"Just a moment," said Pooh, holding up his paw. "*What* did you say? You sneezed as you were about to tell me."

"I *didn't* sneeze."

"Yes, you did, Owl."

"What I *said* was, 'First *Issue* a Reward.'"

"You're doing it again," said Pooh sadly.

"A reward!" said Owl very loudly. "We write a sign that says we will give a large something to anybody who finds Eeyore's tail."

"I see," said Pooh, nodding. "Talking about large somethings, I usually have a small something about now—," and he looked dreamily at the cupboard in Owl's room; "some condensed milk, with maybe a bit of honey—"

"Well, then," said Owl, "we write out this notice, and we put it up all over the Forest."

"A bit of honey," said Bear to himself, "or—or not, it seems." He sighed, and tried very hard to listen to Owl.

But Owl went on and on, using longer and longer words. At last Owl explained that the person to write this sign was Christopher Robin.

"Christopher Robin wrote the signs on my front door. Did you see them, Pooh?"

For some time now, Pooh had not heard anything from Owl. He was saying "Yes" and "No" in turns. Having said, "Yes, yes," last time, he said, "No, not at all," now.

"You didn't see them?" said Owl, surprised.

"Come and look at them now."

So they went outside. Pooh looked at the knocker and the sign below it. He looked at the bell-rope and the sign below it. The more he looked at the bell-rope, the more he felt that he had seen something like it before.

"Beautiful bell-rope, isn't it?" said Owl.

Pooh nodded.

EEYORE LOSES A TAIL

"It reminds me of something," he said, "but I can't remember what. Where did you get it?"

"I found it in the Forest. It was hanging over a bush. I thought somebody lived there, so I rang it very loudly, and it came off the bush. Since nobody wanted it, I took it home, and—"

"Owl," said Pooh seriously, "you made a mistake. Somebody did want it."

"Who?"

"My friend Eeyore. He was—he was fond of it."

"Fond of it?"

"Attached to it," said Winnie-the-Pooh sadly.

* * *

So Pooh took the bell-rope, and returned it to Eeyore.

When Christopher Robin nailed it in its right place, Eeyore danced and waved his tail happily.

53

Winnie-the-Pooh, however, had to hurry home for a snack. Wiping his mouth half an hour later, he sang:

Who found the Tail?
　"I," said Pooh,
"At a quarter to two
　　(Only it was quarter to eleven really),
I found the Tail!"

CHAPTER FIVE

In which Piglet meets a Heffalump

One day, Christopher Robin, Winnie-the-Pooh, and Piglet were talking together. Christopher Robin said: "I saw a Heffalump today, Piglet."

"What was it doing?" asked Piglet.

"Just lumping along," said Christopher Robin. "It didn't see *me*."

"I saw one once," said Piglet. "At least, I think I did."

"So did I," said Pooh, wondering what a Heffalump looked like.

"You don't often see them," said Christopher Robin.

"Not now," said Piglet.

"Not at this time of year," said Pooh.

Then they talked about something else, until it was time for Pooh and Piglet to go home together. At first, they didn't say much. But then they began to talk in a friendly way about this and that. Just as they came to the Six Pine Trees, Pooh looked round to see if anybody was listening. He said in a firm voice:

"Piglet, I have decided something."

"What have you decided, Pooh?"

"I have decided to catch a Heffalump."

Pooh waited for Piglet to say something, but Piglet said nothing. The fact was Piglet wished that *he* had thought about it first.

"I'll use a trap," said Pooh, "It must be a Cunning Trap, so you will have to help me, Piglet."

"I will," said Piglet, feeling happy again. Then he said, "How shall we do it?"

Pooh said, "That's just it. How?" And so they sat down to think.

Pooh's first idea was to dig a Very Deep Pit, and then the Heffalump would fall into the pit, and—

"Why?" said Piglet.

"Why what?" said Pooh.

"Why would he fall in?"

Pooh rubbed his nose. He said that the Heffalump might be walking along, looking at the sky, wondering if it would rain, and so he wouldn't see the Very Deep Pit until it was too late.

Piglet said that this was a very good Trap, but what if it was already raining?

Pooh hadn't thought of that. Then he brightened up. If it were raining already, the Heffalump would be looking at the sky wondering if it would *clear up*, and so he wouldn't see the Very Deep Pit until it was too late.

Now that this had been explained, Piglet thought it was a Cunning Trap.

But there was just one other thing: *Where*

should they dig the Very Deep Pit?

Piglet said the best place would be close to where a Heffalump would be just before he fell into the Pit.

"But then he would see us digging," said Pooh.

"Not if he was looking at the sky."

"He would Suspect," said Pooh, "if he looked down." He added sadly. "It isn't as easy as I thought. Maybe that's why Heffalumps *rarely* get caught."

"That must be it," said Piglet.

They sighed. Pooh said, "If only I could *think* of something!"

"Suppose," he said to Piglet, "*you* wanted to catch *me*, how would you do it?"

"Well," said Piglet, "I should make a Trap, and I should put a Jar of Honey in the Trap, and you would smell it, and you would go in after it, and—"

"And I would go in after it," said Pooh excitedly, "carefully, so I don't hurt myself. I would get to the Jar of Honey, and lick the edges. I'll pretend that there was no more honey.

Piglet Meets a Heffalump

I would walk away, and then I would come back and lick the middle of the jar, and then—"

"Yes, and then I would catch you. Now, what do Heffalumps like? I should think acorns."

Pooh said that Honey was a much more trappy thing than Haycorns. Piglet didn't think so. They were about to argue, when Piglet remembered something. If they used acorns, *he* would have to find the acorns. But if they used honey, then Pooh would have to share his own honey. So Piglet said, "All right, honey then" just as Pooh said "All right, haycorns."

"*I'll* dig the pit, while *you* go and get the honey," said Piglet, as if it were settled.

"Very well," said Pooh, and he stumped off.

At home, he went to his cupboard. He stood on a chair, and took down a large jar of honey from the top shelf. It had HUNNY written on it. But, just to make sure, he

took off the paper cover and looked inside.

It *looked* like honey. "But you never know," said Pooh. "My uncle once saw cheese with this color." So Pooh took a large lick. "Yes," he said, "it is honey. Right down to the bottom of the jar... Unless somebody put cheese at the bottom as a joke. Perhaps I should taste it just a *little* more... just in case Heffalumps *don't* like cheese... Ah!" He gave a deep sigh. "It is honey, all the way down."

Satisfied, he took the jar to Piglet, who was in the Very Deep Pit. Piglet said, "Got it?"

Pooh said, "Yes, but the jar isn't full."

He threw it down to Piglet, and Piglet said, "Is that all?" and Pooh said, "Yes." So Piglet put the jar

at the bottom of the Pit, climbed out, and they went home together.

"Well, good night, Pooh," said Piglet, when they got to Pooh's house. "We'll meet at six o'clock tomorrow morning by the Pine Trees, and see how many Heffalumps are in our Trap."

"Six o'clock, Piglet. And have you got any string?"

"No. Why do you want string?"

"To lead them home with."

"Oh!...I *think* Heffalumps come if you whistle."

"Some do and some don't. You never know with Heffalumps. Well, good night!"

"Good night!"

And Piglet went to his house, while Pooh prepared for bed.

Some hours later, Pooh awoke with a sinking feeling. That sinking feeling meant that *he was hungry.* He went to his cupboard, stood on a chair, reached for the top shelf, and found— nothing.

"That's funny," he thought. "I know I had a jar of honey there. A full jar of honey. It had

HUNNY written on it, so that I should know it was honey. That's very funny." And then he began to wander up and down, murmuring to himself. Like this:

It's very, very funny,
'Cos I *know* I had some honey;
'Cos it had a label on.
    Saying HUNNY.
A goloptious full-up pot too,
And I don't know where it's got to,
No, I don't know where it's gone—
    Well, it's funny.

And then suddenly he remembered. He had put it into the Cunning Trap to catch the Heffalump.

"Bother!" said Pooh. He went back to bed.

But he couldn't sleep. He tried Counting Sheep, but it was no good. So he tried counting Heffalumps. And that was worse. Because every Heffalump he counted was *eating all his honey*. He was miserable. When the five hundred and eighty-seventh Heffalump licked its jaws, and

Piglet Meets a Heffalump

said to itself, "Very good honey, I've never tasted better," Pooh could bear it no longer.

He jumped out of bed, and ran to the Six Pine Trees.

The sun was just waking up over the Hundred Acre
Wood. There was little light, and so the Very Deep Pit seemed deeper and Pooh's jar of honey looked like a mysterious shape and nothing more. But as he got nearer, his nose told him

that it was indeed honey. His tongue came out, ready to taste it.

"Bother!" said Pooh, as he got his nose inside the jar. "A Heffalump has been eating it!" And then he paused and said, "Oh, no, *I* did. I forgot."

Indeed, he had eaten most of it. But there was a little left at the bottom of the jar, so he pushed his head in, and began to lick...

Soon Piglet woke up and said to himself, "Oh!" Then he said bravely, "Yes." But he didn't feel brave, because the word jiggeting in his brain was "Heffalumps."

What was a Heffalump like?

Was it Fierce?

Did it come when you whistled?

Was it Fond of Pigs?

If it was Fond of Pigs, did it matter *what sort of Pig?*

If it was Fierce with Pigs, would it matter *if the Pig had a grandfather called TRESPASSERS WILLIAM?*

Piglet Meets a Heffalump

He didn't know... and he was going to see his first Heffalump in an hour!

Of course Pooh would be there... But, maybe Heffalumps were Very Fierce with Pigs *and* Bears? Maybe he should pretend he had a headache, and couldn't go out this morning. But what if it was a fine day, and there was no Heffalump in the trap? He would be in bed all morning, wasting his time for nothing. What should he do?

Piglet then had a Clever Idea. He would go to the Six Pine Trees, look into the Trap, and firstly see if there *was* a Heffalump there. And if there was, he would go back to bed. If there wasn't, he wouldn't.

So off he went. At first he thought that there wouldn't be a Heffalump in the Trap. Then as he got nearer, he thought that there would be one, because he could hear it heffalumping about.

"Oh, dear, oh, dear, oh, dear!" said Piglet. He wanted to run away. But having got so near, he felt that he must see what a Heffalump was like. So he went to the side of the Trap and looked in...

Winnie-the-Pooh had been trying to get the honey-jar off his head. The more he shook it, however, the more it stuck. "*Bother!*" he said, and "*Oh, help!*" and, mostly, "*Ow!*" He tried to climb out of the Trap, but as he couldn't see anything, he couldn't find his way. So at last he lifted his head, and roared loudly in Sadness and Despair... it was at that moment that Piglet looked down.

"Help, help!" cried Piglet, "a Horrible Heffalump!" He ran off, crying, "Help, help, a Herrible Hoffalump! Hoff, Hoff, a Hellible Horralump!"

He didn't stop crying

Piglet Meets a Heffalump

and running until he got to
Christopher Robin's house.

"What's the matter, Piglet?"
said Christopher Robin.

"Heff," said Piglet, breathing
so hard that he could hardly
speak, "a Heff—a Heff—a Heffalump."

"Where?"

"Up there," said Piglet, waving his paw.

"What did it look like?"

"Like—like—It had the biggest head you ever saw, Christopher Robin. A great enormous thing, like—a huge big—well,—like an enormous big—like a jar."

"Well," said Christopher Robin, "I shall go and look at it. Come on."

So off they went...

"I can hear it, can't you?"
said Piglet anxiously, as they
got near.

"I can hear *something*,"
said Christopher Robin.

It was Pooh bumping
his head against a tree-root.

"There!" said Piglet. "Isn't it *awful*?" And he held on tight to Christopher Robin's hand.

Suddenly Christopher Robin began to laugh...and he laughed...and laughed. And while he was still laughing—*Crash* went the Heffalump's head against the tree-root, *Smash* went the jar, and out came Pooh's head...

Piglet saw what a Foolish Piglet he had been. He was so ashamed that he ran straight home and went to bed. But Christopher Robin and Pooh went home to have breakfast.

"Oh, Bear!" said Christopher Robin. "How I do love you!"

"So do I," said Pooh.

CHAPTER SIX

In which Eeyore has a birthday and gets two presents

Eeyore, the old grey Donkey, looked at himself in the water.

"Pathetic," he said.

He walked slowly to the other side of the stream. Then he looked at himself in the water again.

"Of course," he said. "Pathetic from *this* side too."

There was a noise from behind him, and Pooh appeared.

"Good morning, Eeyore," said Pooh.

"Good morning, Pooh Bear," said Eeyore gloomily. "If it is a good morning."

"What's the matter?"

"Nothing, Pooh Bear. We can't all, and some of us don't. That's all."

EEYORE HAS A BIRTHDAY

"Can't all *what*?" said Pooh, rubbing his nose.

"Happiness. Song-and-dance. Round the mulberry bush."

"Oh!" said Pooh. "What mulberry bush?"

"Bon-hommy," Eeyore continued gloomily. "A French word meaning bonhommy," he explained. "I'm not complaining, but There It Is."

Pooh sat down on a large stone, and tried to understand Eeyore's words. It sounded like a riddle. He was not good at riddles because he was a Bear of Very Little Brain. So he sang *Cottleston Pie* instead:

Cottleston, Cottleston, Cottleston Pie,
A fly can't bird, but a bird can fly.
Ask me a riddle and I reply:
"*Cottleston, Cottleston, Cottleston Pie.*"

71

That was the first verse. Eeyore didn't say he didn't like it, so Pooh kindly sang the second verse to him:

Cottleston, Cottleston, Cottleston Pie,
A fish can't whistle and neither can I.
Ask me a riddle and I reply:
"Cottleston, Cottleston, Cottleston Pie."

"That's right," said Eeyore. "Sing. Umty-tiddly, umty-too. Enjoy yourself."

"I am," said Pooh. "But you seem so sad, Eeyore."

"Sad? Why should I be sad? It's my birthday. The happiest day of the year."

"Your birthday?" said Pooh, surprised.

"Of course. Can't you see? Look at all my presents. Look at the birthday cake. Candles and pink sugar."

Pooh looked—first to the right, then to the left.

"Presents?" said Pooh. "Birthday cake? *Where?*"

Eeyore has a Birthday

"Can't you see them?"

"No," said Pooh.

"Neither can I. It's a joke," Eeyore explained. "Ha ha!"

Pooh scratched his head, confused.

"But is it really your birthday?" he asked.

"It is."

"Oh! Well, happy birthday, Eeyore."

"And happy birthday to you, Pooh Bear."

"But it isn't *my* birthday."

"No, it's mine."

"But you said 'Happy'—"

"Well, why not? Do you want to be sad on my birthday? It's bad enough," said Eeyore, almost breaking down, "being sad myself, with no presents and no cake and no candles, because no one remembered my birthday—"

This was too much for Pooh. "Stay there!" he called to Eeyore. Pooh hurried home. He felt that he must get poor Eeyore a present at once.

Outside his house he found Piglet, trying to reach the knocker.

"Hallo, Piglet," he said.

"Hallo, Pooh," said Piglet.

"What are *you* trying to do?"

"I was trying to reach the knocker," said Piglet. "I just came round—"

"Let me do it for you," said Pooh kindly. He reached up and knocked at the door. "I just met Eeyore," he began, "and poor Eeyore is Very Sad because it's his birthday, and nobody remembered. He's very Gloomy and—Why hasn't anyone answered the door?" He knocked again.

"But, Pooh," said Piglet, "it's your house!"

"Oh!" said Pooh. "That's right. Well, let's go in."

The first thing Pooh did was to see if he had a jar of honey left. He did have one, so he took it down.

Eeyore has a Birthday

"I'm giving this to Eeyore," he explained, "as a present. What is *your* present?"

"Couldn't I give it too?" said Piglet. "From both of us?"

"No," said Pooh. "That would *not* be a good plan."

"All right, then, I'll give him a balloon. I've got one left from my party. Shall I go and get it now?"

"That is a *very* good idea. A balloon will cheer Eeyore up."

So Piglet ran home; and Pooh went the opposite way with his jar of honey.

It was a long journey for Pooh. Halfway through, Pooh felt a funny feeling in his body. It was as if somebody were saying, "Pooh, it's time for a little something."

"Dear, dear," said Pooh, "I didn't know it was so late." He sat down and opened his jar of honey. "Luckily I have this." And he began to eat.

"Now," he thought, as he licked the last drop, "where was I going? Ah, yes, Eeyore."

Then, he remembered. He had eaten Eeyore's birthday present!

"*Bother!*" said Pooh. "What *shall* I do? I *must* give him *something*."

At first he couldn't think of anything. Then he thought: "Well, it's a nice pot, even if there's no honey in it. I could wash it, and have Owl write '*Happy Birthday*' on it. And Eeyore could keep things in it, which might be Useful." So Pooh went to find Owl for help.

"Good morning, Owl," he said.

"Good morning, Pooh," said Owl.

"It's Eeyore's birthday today," said Pooh.

"Oh, is it?"

"I'm giving him a Useful Pot, and I wanted to ask you—"

"Is this it?" said Owl, taking it from Pooh. "Somebody has been keeping honey in it."

"You can keep *anything* in it," said Pooh. "because it's Very Useful. And I wanted to ask—"

"You should write '*Happy Birthday*' on it."

"*That* was what I wanted to ask you," said Pooh. "My spelling is Wobbly and the letters get in the wrong places. Would *you* write 'Happy Birthday' for me?"

"It's a nice pot," said Owl, looking at it all round. "Couldn't I give it too? From both of us?"

"No," said Pooh. "That would *not* be a good plan. Now I'll just wash it first, and then you can write on it."

While Pooh washed and dried the pot, Owl wondered how to spell "birthday."

"Can you read, Pooh?" he asked nervously. "Could you read the sign outside my door, for example?"

"Yes, because Christopher Robin told me what it said."

"Well, then, I'll tell you what *this* says."

So . . . Owl wrote:

HIPY PAPY BTHUTHDTH THUTHDA BTHUTHDY.

Pooh admired the words.

"I wrote 'Happy Birthday'," said Owl.

"It's nice and long," said Pooh, impressed.

"Well, *actually*, I wrote 'A Very Happy Birthday with love from Pooh.' That's why it's all nice and long."

"Oh, I see," said Pooh.

While all this was happening, Piglet had found his balloon for Eeyore at home.

Piglet then ran as fast as he could to see Eeyore, thinking how he would like to be the first one to give Eeyore a present. Imagining how happy Eeyore would be, he didn't look where he was going... and suddenly he tripped, and fell on his face.

BANG!!!???***!!!

Piglet lay there, wondering what had happened. He thought that maybe he had blown up. Maybe he was now on the moon, and would never see Christopher Robin or Pooh or Eeyore again. And then he thought, "Even if I'm on the moon, I can't lie on the ground forever," so he stood up carefully. He looked around.

He was still in the Forest!

"That's funny," he thought. "I wonder what that bang was. And where's my balloon? What's this small piece of rag?"

It was the balloon!

"Oh, dear!" said Piglet. "Oh, dearie, dear! It's too late. I can't go back, and I don't have another balloon. Maybe Eeyore doesn't *like* balloons so *very* much."

He walked on sadly until he found Eeyore.

"Good morning, Eeyore," said Piglet.

"Good morning, Little Piglet," said Eeyore. "If it *is* a good morning."

"Happy birthday," said Piglet.

Eeyore stopped and turned to stare at Piglet.

"Say that again," he said.

"Hap—"

"Wait a moment."

He lifted a leg carefully up to his ear. "It's so I can hear better," he explained.

"There, that's done! Now, what were you saying?" He pushed his ear forward with his hoof.

"Happy birthday," said Piglet again.

"Meaning me?"

"Of course, Eeyore."

"Me having a real birthday?"

"Yes, Eeyore, and I have a present."

Eeyore took down his right hoof from his right ear. Then he put up his left hoof.

"Let me try this ear," he said. "What did you say?"

"A present," said Piglet loudly.

"Meaning me again?"

"Yes."

"My birthday still?"

"Yes, Eeyore. I brought you a balloon."

"A *balloon*?" said Eeyore. "One of those big colored things you blow up? Happiness, song-and-dance, round the mulberry bush?"

"Yes, but—I'm very sorry, Eeyore—but when I ran to bring it to you, I fell down."

"Dear, dear, how unlucky! Did you hurt yourself, Little Piglet?"

"No, but I—I—oh, Eeyore, I burst the balloon!"

There was a very long silence.

"My birthday balloon?" said Eeyore at last.

"Yes, Eeyore," said Piglet, sniffing. "Here it is. Hap—happy birthday." And he gave Eeyore the small piece of rag.

"Is this my present?" said Eeyore, surprised.

Piglet nodded.

"The balloon?"

"Yes."

"Thank you, Piglet," said Eeyore. "What color was this balloon when it—when it *was* a balloon?"

"Red."

"Red," he murmured to himself. "My favorite color... How big was it?"

"About as big as me."

"About as big as Piglet," he said to himself sadly. "My favorite size. Well, well."

Piglet felt awful, and didn't know what to say. He opened his mouth to say something, but then he heard a shout from far away. It was Pooh.

"Happy birthday," called Pooh.

"Thank you, Pooh," said Eeyore gloomily.

"I've brought you a little present," said Pooh excitedly.

Pooh splashed across the stream to Eeyore.

"It's a Useful Pot," said Pooh. "Here it is. It has 'A Very Happy Birthday with love from Pooh' written on it. And it's for putting things in there!"

When Eeyore saw the pot, he became excited.

"Why!" he said. "I believe my Balloon will fit into that Pot!"

"Oh, no, Eeyore," said Pooh. "Balloons are too big to fit into Pots. You have to hold the balloon—"

"Not mine," said Eeyore proudly. "Look, Piglet!"

And as Piglet turned sadly round, Eeyore picked the balloon up with his teeth, and placed it carefully in the pot. He picked it out and put it on the ground, then picked it up again and put it carefully back.

"So it does!" said Pooh. "It fits!"

"And it comes out too!" said Piglet.

"Yes," said Eeyore. "It goes in and out perfectly."

"I'm very glad," said Pooh happily, "that I gave you a Useful Pot to put things in."

"I'm very glad," said Piglet happily, "that I gave you Something to put in a Useful Pot."

But Eeyore wasn't listening. He was taking the balloon out, and putting it back in, feeling so very happy...

Winnie-the-Pooh

"Did *I* give him anything?" asked Christopher Robin sadly.

"Of course you did," I said. "You gave him—don't you remember—a little—a little—"

"I gave him a box of paints."

"That was it."

"Why didn't I give it to him in the morning?"

"You were busy getting his party ready. He had a cake with icing on top, and three candles, and his name in pink sugar, and—"

"Yes, *I* remember," said Christopher Robin.

CHAPTER SEVEN

In which Kanga and Baby Roo come to the Forest, and Piglet has a bath

Nobody knew where they came from, but there they were in the Forest: Kanga and Baby Roo. When Pooh asked Christopher Robin, "How did they come here?" Christopher Robin said, "The Usual Way, if you know what I mean, Pooh." Pooh, who didn't know what that meant, said "Oh!" He went to his friend Piglet to see if *he* knew. And at Piglet's house he found Rabbit. So they all talked about it together.

"This is what I don't like about it," said Rabbit. "Here we are—you, Pooh, and you, Piglet, and Me—and suddenly—"

"And Eeyore," said Pooh.

"And Eeyore—"

"And Owl," said Pooh.

"And Owl—and suddenly—"

"Oh, and Eeyore," said Pooh. "I was forgetting *him*."

"Here—we—are," said Rabbit very slowly and carefully, "all—of—us, and then, suddenly, we wake up, and what do we find? Strange Animals! An animal who carries her family in her pocket! What if *I* carried *my* family in *my* pocket, how many pockets should I have?"

"Sixteen," said Piglet.

"Seventeen, I believe?" said Rabbit. "And one more for a handkerchief—that's eighteen. Eighteen pockets in one suit!"

There was a long and thoughtful silence ...

"The question is, what do we do about Kanga?" said Piglet.

"The best way," said Rabbit, "would be this. We should steal Baby Roo and hide him, and then when Kanga says, 'Where's Baby Roo?' we say, '*Aha!*'"

"*Aha!*" said Pooh, practicing. "*Aha! Aha!* ... Of course, we could say '*Aha!*' even if we didn't steal Baby Roo."

"Pooh," said Rabbit kindly, "you don't have any brain."

"I know," said Pooh.

"We say '*Aha!*' because it means 'We'll tell you where Baby Roo is, if you promise to go away from the Forest and never come back.' Now let me think."

"There's just one thing," said Piglet. "Christopher Robin said that a Kanga was One of the Fiercer Animals. I am not frightened of regular Fierce Animals, but if One of the Fiercer Animals Lost Its Baby, it becomes as fierce as Two of the Fiercer Animals. And then maybe '*Aha!*' is a *foolish* thing to say."

"Piglet," said Rabbit, "you are not very brave."

"It is hard to be brave," said Piglet, "when you're only a Very Small Animal."

Rabbit said: "Even if you are a very small animal, you will be very Useful in our adventure."

Piglet was so excited at the idea of being Useful that he forgot to be frightened.

"I suppose *I* can't be useful?" said Pooh sadly.

"Never mind, Pooh," said Piglet comfortingly.

"Another time maybe."

"Without Pooh," said Rabbit seriously, "this adventure would be impossible."

"Oh!" said Piglet, and tried not to look disappointed.

But Pooh said proudly to himself, "Impossible without Me!"

"Now listen," said Rabbit. He had written down a plan. Pooh and Piglet sat and listened, excited. This was what Rabbit read out:

PLAN TO CAPTURE BABY ROO

1. *General Thoughts*. Kanga runs faster than any of Us, even Me.
2. *More General Thoughts*. Kanga is always watching Baby Roo, except when he's safe in her pocket.

3. *Therefore.* If we want to capture Baby Roo, we must have an Early Start, because Kanga runs faster than any of Us, even Me. (*See* 1.)
4. *A Thought.* If Roo jumped out of Kanga's pocket and Piglet jumped in, Kanga wouldn't know the difference, because Piglet is a Very Small Animal.
5. Like Roo.
6. But Kanga would have to be looking the other way, so she would not see Piglet jumping in.
7. *See* 2.
8. *Another Thought.* If Pooh talked to her excitedly, she might look the other way for a moment.
9. And then I could run away with Roo.
10. Quickly.
11. *And Kanga wouldn't discover the difference until Afterwards.*

Rabbit read this proudly, and for a while nobody said anything. And then Piglet managed to say quietly:

"And—Afterwards?"

"What do you mean?"

"When Kanga *does* Discover the Difference?"

"Then we all say '*Aha!*'"

"All three of us?"

"Yes."

"Oh!"

"Why, what's wrong, Piglet?"

"Nothing," said Piglet, "as long as *we all* say it. I don't want to say '*Aha!*' by myself."

"All right. Well, Pooh? Do you know what to do?"

"Not yet," said Pooh Bear. "What *do* I do?"

"Well, you have to talk a lot to Kanga so she doesn't see anything."

"Oh! What about?"

"Anything."

"Can I tell her a poem?"

"Yes, of course," said Rabbit. "Wonderful. Now let's go."

So they went out to look for Kanga.

Kanga and Roo were having a quiet afternoon together. Baby Roo was practicing small jumps in the sand. Kanga was walking around saying "Just one more jump, dear, and then we must go home."

At that moment, Pooh appeared.

"Good afternoon, Kanga."

"Good afternoon, Pooh."

"Look at me jumping," squeaked Roo.

"Hallo, Roo!"

"We were just going home," said Kanga.

"Good afternoon, Rabbit. Good afternoon, Piglet."

Rabbit and Piglet said "Good afternoon," and "Hallo, Roo." Roo asked them to watch him jump, so they stayed and watched.

And Kanga watched too...

"Oh, Kanga," said Pooh, after Rabbit had winked at him twice, "Do you like Poetry?"

"Not really," said Kanga.

"Oh!" said Pooh.

"Roo, dear, just one more jump and then we must go home."

There was a short silence while Roo continued jumping.

"Go on," said Rabbit in a loud whisper.

"I made up a little poem as I came here," said Pooh. "It went like this. Er—now let me see—"

"Lovely!" said Kanga. "Now Roo, dear—"

"You'll like this piece of poetry," said Rabbit.

"Don't miss any of it," said Piglet.

"Oh, yes," said Kanga, but she was still looking at Baby Roo.

"*How* did it go, Pooh?" said Rabbit.

Pooh gave a little cough and began.

LINES WRITTEN BY A BEAR OF
VERY LITTLE BRAIN

On Monday, when the sun is hot
I wonder to myself a lot:
"Now is it true, or is it not,
"That what is which and which is what?"

On Tuesday, when it hails and snows,
The feeling on me grows and grows
That hardly anybody knows
If those are these or these are those.

On Wednesday, when the sky is blue,
And I have nothing else to do,
I sometimes wonder if it's true
That who is what and what is who.

On Thursday, when it starts to freeze
And hoar-frost twinkles on the trees,
How very readily one sees
That these are whose—but whose are these?

On Friday—

Kanga and Baby Roo

"How nice," said Kanga. She did not wait to hear what happened on Friday. "Just one more jump, Roo, dear, and then we *must* be going home."

"Talking of Poetry," said Pooh quickly, "have you ever noticed that tree over there?"

"Where?" said Kanga. "Now, Roo—"

"Over there," said Pooh, pointing behind Kanga's back.

"No," said Kanga. "Now jump in, Roo, dear, and we'll go home."

"You should look at that tree over there," said Rabbit. "Shall I help you in, Roo?" And he picked up Roo in his paws.

"I can see a bird in the tree," said Pooh. "Or is it a fish?"

"You should see that bird from here," said Rabbit. "Unless it's a fish."

Finally, Kanga turned her head to look. The moment her head was turned, Rabbit said in a loud voice "In you go, Roo!" and Piglet jumped into Kanga's pocket. Rabbit ran off with Roo in his paws, as fast as he could.

"Why, where's Rabbit?" said Kanga, turning round again. "Are you all right, Roo, dear?"

Piglet made a squeaky Roo-noise.

"Rabbit had to go away," said Pooh. "I think he had something he had to do suddenly."

"And Piglet?"

"I think Piglet thought of something at the same time. Suddenly."

"Well, we must go home," said Kanga. "Goodbye, Pooh." And in three large jumps she was gone.

Pooh looked after her as she went.

"I wish I could jump like that," he thought.

Piglet wished that Kanga couldn't jump.

Kanga and Baby Roo

He had once also wished that he could fly, but now that he was at the bottom of Kanga's pocket, he thought,

"If ^{this} is _{flying} I ^{shall} never ^{like} ^{it} very _{much.}"

He was saying, "*Ooooooo-ow, Ooooooo-ow, Ooooooo-ow*" all the way to Kanga's house.

As soon as Kanga arrived home, she saw what had happened. She wasn't worried because she knew Christopher Robin would never let anything bad happen to Roo. So she said to herself, "If they are playing a joke, I will play a joke too."

"Now, Roo, dear," she said, as she took Piglet out of her pocket. "Bedtime."

"*Aha!*" said Piglet. It wasn't a very good "*Aha!*"

Piglet looked round for the others.

But the others weren't there. Rabbit was playing with Baby Roo in his own house, loving him more and more every minute. And Pooh, who had decided to be a Kanga, was still practicing jumps.

"I think," said Kanga, "that it would be a good idea to have a *cold* bath first. Would you like that, Roo, dear?"

Piglet had never really liked baths. He tried to sound brave when he said:

"Kanga, it's time to tell you the truth."

"Funny little Roo," said Kanga, as she got the bath-water ready.

"I am *not* Roo," said Piglet loudly. "I am Piglet!"

KANGA AND BABY ROO

"Yes, dear, yes," said Kanga. "And imitating Piglet's voice too! How clever." She took a large bar of yellow soap from the cupboard.

"Can't you *see*?" shouted Piglet. "*Look* at me!"

"I *am* looking, Roo, dear," said Kanga, rather severely. "Now, into the bath, and don't make me tell you again."

Before he knew it, Kanga began washing him.

"*Ow!*" cried Piglet. "Let me out! I'm Piglet!"

"Don't open your mouth, dear, or the soap goes in," said Kanga. "There! See?"

"You—you—you did it on purpose," said Piglet . . . and then got more soap in his mouth.

"Don't say anything, dear," said Kanga. In another minute Piglet was out of the bath, and being dried with a towel.

At that moment there was a knock at the door.

"Come in," said Kanga, and in came Christopher Robin.

"Christopher Robin!" cried Piglet. "Tell Kanga who I am! She keeps saying I'm Roo. I'm *not* Roo, am I?"

Christopher Robin looked at him carefully, and shook his head.

"You can't be Roo," he said, "because I've just seen Roo in Rabbit's house."

"Well!" said Kanga. "I can't believe I made this mistake."

"I told you so!" said Piglet. "I'm Piglet."

Christopher Robin shook his head again.

"Oh, you're not Piglet," he said. "I know Piglet well, and he is *not* this color."

KANGA AND BABY ROO

"I knew it wasn't Piglet," said Kanga. "I wonder who it is."

"Maybe it's one of Pooh's family," said Christopher Robin. "Maybe a nephew or an uncle?"

Kanga agreed, and said that they should call it by a name.

"I shall call it Pootel," said Christopher Robin. "Henry Pootel."

And just when it was decided, Henry Pootel jumped out of Kanga's arms. He ran faster than he ever had in his life.

When he was close to his house, he stopped running, and rolled the rest of the way home to get his own color again ...

So Kanga and Roo stayed in the Forest. Every Tuesday after that Roo spent the day with his great friend Rabbit, Kanga spent the day with her great friend Pooh, teaching him to jump, and Piglet spent the day with his great friend Christopher Robin. So they were all happy again.

CHAPTER EIGHT

In which Christopher Robin
leads an expotition to the North Pole

One fine day Pooh stumped up to the top of the Forest to find his friend Christopher Robin. At breakfast that morning (a simple meal of jam with a honeycomb or two) he had suddenly thought of a new song. It began like this:

"Sing Ho! for the life of a Bear."

Then he thought to himself, "That's a very good start for a song, but what about the rest?" He tried singing "Ho," two or three times, but it didn't help. "Very well, then," he said, "I shall sing that first line twice. Maybe if I sing it very quickly, I will suddenly start singing the third and fourth lines. That will be a Good Song. Now then:"

Sing Ho! for the life of a Bear!
Sing Ho! for the life of a Bear!
I don't much mind if it rains or snows,
'Cos I've got a lot of honey on my nice new nose!
I don't much care if it snows or thaws,
'Cos I've got a lot of honey on my nice clean paws!
Sing Ho! for a Bear!
Sing Ho! for a Pooh!
And I'll have a little something in an hour or two!

He was so happy with this song that he sang it all the way to the top of the Forest.

Christopher Robin was sitting outside his door, putting on his Big Boots. As soon as Pooh saw the Big Boots, he knew that an Adventure was going to happen.

"Good morning, Christopher Robin," he called out.

"Hallo, Pooh Bear. I can't get this boot on."

"That's bad," said Pooh.

"Could you kindly lean against me? I keep pulling so hard that I fall over backwards."

Pooh sat down, pushed hard against Christopher Robin's back, and Christopher

Robin pushed hard against Pooh's. Christopher Robin pulled and pulled at his boot until it came on.

"And that's that," said Pooh. "What do we do next?"

"We are going on an Expedition," said Christopher Robin, as he got up. "Thank you, Pooh."

"An Expotition?" said Pooh, excited. "I don't think I've been on one before. Where are we going on this Expotition?"

"Expedition, silly old Bear. It has an 'x' in it."

"Oh!" said Pooh. "I know." But he didn't really.

"We're going to discover the North Pole."

"Oh!" said Pooh again. "What *is* the North Pole?"

"It's just a thing you discover," said Christopher Robin, not sure himself.

"Oh! I see," said Pooh. "Are bears any good at discovering it?"

"Of course they are. And Rabbit and Kanga and all of you. That's what an Expedition means. A long line of everybody. You should tell the others to get ready. And we must all bring Provisions."

"Bring what?"

"Things to eat."

"Oh!" said Pooh happily. "I thought you said Provisions. I'll go and tell them." And he stumped off.

The first person he met was Rabbit.

"Hallo, Rabbit," he said, "We're all going on an Expotition with Christopher Robin!"

"What is an Expotition?"

"A sort of boat, I think," said Pooh.

"Oh!"

"Yes. And we're going to discover a Pole, or maybe a Mole? Anyhow we're going to discover it."

"Are we?" said Rabbit.

"Yes. And we have to bring Pro-things to eat. Now I'm going to tell Piglet. Tell Kanga, please?"

He left Rabbit and hurried to Piglet's house. Piglet was at the door of his house, blowing happily at a dandelion, when Pooh appeared.

"Piglet," said Pooh excitedly, "we're all going on an Expotition, with things to eat. To discover something."

"To discover what?" said Piglet, nervously.

"Oh! just something."

"Nothing fierce?"

"Christopher Robin didn't say anything about fierce. He just said it had an 'x'."

"It isn't their necks I mind," said Piglet earnestly. "It's their teeth. But if Christopher Robin is coming I don't mind anything."

Soon they were all at the top of the Forest, and the Expotition started. First came Christopher Robin and Rabbit, then Piglet and Pooh; then Kanga, with Roo in her pocket, and Owl; then Eeyore; and, at the end, in a long line, all of Rabbit's friends and family.

"I didn't invite them," explained Rabbit. "They just came. They always do. They can walk at the end, after Eeyore."

"I'm not all right with this," said Eeyore, "I didn't want to come on this Expo—what Pooh said. I only came because I was asked to. And if I am at the end of the Expo—what Pooh said—then let me *be* the end. But if, every time I want to rest I have to wave along all of Rabbit's friends and family, then this isn't an Expo—whatever it is—at all. It's simply a Confused Noise."

"I see what Eeyore means," said Owl. "If you ask me—"

"I'm not asking anybody," said Eeyore. "I'm telling everybody. We can look for the North Pole, or we can do something else. It's all the same to me."

EXPOTITION TO THE NORTH POLE

There was a shout from the top of the line.

"Come on!" called Christopher Robin.

"Come on!" called Pooh and Piglet.

"Come on!" called Owl.

"We're starting," said Rabbit. "I must go." And he hurried to the front of the Expotition with Christopher Robin.

So off they went to discover the Pole. As they walked, they talked to each other about this and that. All except Pooh, who was making up a song.

"This is the first verse," he said to Piglet, when he had finished the song.

"First verse of what?"

"My song."

"What song?"

"Well, if you listen, Piglet, you'll hear it."

Pooh began to sing.

They all went off to discover the Pole,
    Owl and Piglet and Rabbit and all;
It's a Thing you Discover, as I've been tole
    By Owl and Piglet and Rabbit and all.
Eeyore, Christopher Robin and Pooh

And Rabbit's relations all went too—
And where the Pole was none of them knew...
 Sing Hey! for Owl and Rabbit and all!

"Hush!" said Christopher Robin, turning to Pooh, "we're coming to a Dangerous Place."

"Hush!" said Pooh, turning to Piglet.

"Hush!" said Piglet to Kanga.

"Hush!" said Kanga to Owl.

"Hush!" said Owl to Eeyore.

"*Hush!*" said Eeyore in a terrible voice to all of Rabbit's friends and family, and "Hush!" they said to each other, until it got to the last one of all. And the last and smallest of Rabbit's friends and family was so sad to find that the whole

Expotition to the North Pole

Expotition was saying "Hush!" to *him*, that he hid his head in a hole in the ground. He stayed there for two days, and  then went home. He lived quietly with his Aunt forever after that. His name was Alexander Beetle.

They arrived at a stream, and Christopher Robin saw how dangerous it was.

"It's the type of place," he explained, "for an Ambush."

"What sort of bush?" whispered Pooh to Piglet. "A gorse-bush?"

"My dear Pooh," said Owl proudly, "don't you know what an Ambush is?"

"Owl," said Piglet, crossly, "Pooh's whisper was a private whisper, and there was no need—"

"An Ambush," said Owl, "is a sort of Surprise."

"A gorse-bush can be a surprise," said Pooh.

"No, if people jump out at you suddenly, that's an Ambush," continued Owl.

Pooh, who now knew what an Ambush

was, said that a gorse-bush had jumped at him suddenly one day when he fell off a tree.

"We are not *talking* about gorse-bushes," said Owl a little crossly.

"I am," said Pooh.

Not long after, they arrived at a place where they could sit on grass and rest. Christopher Robin called "Halt!" and they all sat down and rested.

"I think," said Christopher Robin, "that we should eat all our Provisions now. So we don't have to carry them anymore."

"Eat all our what?" said Pooh.

"Our food," said Piglet.

"That's a good idea," said Pooh, and he began to eat.

"Do you all have something?" asked Christopher Robin.

"All except me," said Eeyore. He looked round sadly. "Is anyone sitting on a thistle?"

"I think I am," said Pooh. "Ow!" He got up, and looked behind him. "Yes, I was."

"Thank you, Pooh." Eeyore moved to where Pooh was, and began to eat.

As soon as Christopher Robin had finished his lunch he and Rabbit walked away from the others.

"I didn't want the others to hear," said Christopher Robin.

"Of course," said Rabbit, looking important.

"I wondered—It's only—Rabbit, what does the North Pole *look* like?"

"Well," said Rabbit, "Now you're asking me."

"I did know once, but I forgot," said Christopher Robin.

"It's funny," said Rabbit, "I've forgotten too. But I also did know *once*."

"Maybe it's just a pole in the ground?"

"It must be a pole," said Rabbit, "because

it's called a pole. And it must be in the ground, because where else can it be?"

"Yes, that's what I thought."

"The only thing," said Rabbit, "is, *where is it?*"

"That's what we're looking for," said Christopher Robin.

They went back to the others. Roo was washing his face and paws in the stream. Kanga explained to everybody proudly that this was the first time Roo had washed his face by himself.

Suddenly, there was a squeak from Roo, a splash, and a loud cry of fright from Kanga.

"Roo's fallen in!" cried Rabbit, and he and Christopher Robin ran to the rescue.

"Are you all right, Roo, dear?" called Kanga, frightened.

"Yes!" said Roo. "Look at me swimming—" and down he went over the next waterfall into another pool.

Everybody was doing something to help. Piglet was jumping up and down and making "Oo, I say" noises; Owl was explaining that in a case of Sudden and Temporary Immersion

the Important Thing was to keep the Head Above Water; Kanga was jumping along the bank, saying "Are you *sure* you're all right, Roo dear?" And Roo was answering "Look at me swimming!" Eeyore had turned round and hung his tail over the first pool that Roo fell into, and said, "Catch my tail, little Roo, and you'll be all right." Christopher Robin and Rabbit ran past Eeyore, and called out to the others in front of them.

"Get something across the stream farther down!" called Rabbit.

Pooh was two pools below Roo. He stood with a long pole in his paws, and Kanga helped hold one end of it.

They held the pole across the pool. Roo drifted up against it, and climbed out.

"Did you see me swimming?" squeaked Roo. Kanga scolded him and rubbed him dry. "Pooh, did you see me swimming? That's called swimming. Rabbit, did you see what I was doing? Swimming! Christopher Robin, did you see me—"

But Christopher Robin wasn't listening. He was looking at Pooh.

"Pooh," he said, "where did you find that pole?" Pooh looked at the pole in his hands.

"I just found it," he said. "I thought it might be useful. I just picked it up."

Expotition to the North Pole

"Pooh," said Christopher Robin in a serious voice, "the Expedition is over. You have found the North Pole!"

"Oh!" said Pooh.

Eeyore was sitting with his tail in the water when they all returned to him.

"Tell Roo to be quick," he said. "I don't want to complain, but my tail is getting cold."

"Here I am!" squeaked Roo.

"Oh, there you are."

Eeyore took his tail out of the water, and moved it from side to side.

"I thought so," he said. "It has lost all feeling."

"Poor old Eeyore! I'll dry it for you," said Christopher Robin. He took out a handkerchief and rubbed it dry.

"Thank you, Christopher Robin. You're the only one who seems to understand tails."

"Is *that* better?" asked Christopher Robin.

"It's feeling more like a tail now."

"Hullo, Eeyore," said Pooh, coming up to them with his pole.

"Hullo, Pooh."

"Pooh's found the North Pole," said Christopher Robin. "Isn't that lovely?"

Pooh looked modestly down.

They stuck the pole in the ground, and Christopher Robin tied a message on to it:

EXPOTITION TO THE NORTH POLE

NorTH PoLE
DICSovERED By
PooH
PooH FouND IT

Then they all went home. And I think, but I am not sure, that Roo had a hot bath and went straight to bed. But Pooh went back to his own house, and felt very proud of what he had done. So he had a little something to eat.

CHAPTER NINE

In which Piglet is entirely surrounded by water

It rained and it rained and it rained. In all of Piglet's three—or maybe four?—years of life, he had never seen so much rain. Days and days of rain.

"If only," he thought, "I had been in Pooh's house, or Christopher Robin's house, or Rabbit's house when it began to rain, then I would have some Company. But I'm here all alone, with nothing to do except wonder when it will stop." It would have been wonderful to talk with his friends. It wasn't much good when something exciting like a flood happened, if you couldn't share it with someone.

For it was rather exciting. Water had filled up and spilled out of ditches, streams, and even the river where they played. Piglet was beginning to

Surrounded by Water

wonder whether it would be coming into *his* bed soon.

"It's a little Worrying," he said to himself, "to be a Very Small Animal Entirely Surrounded

by Water. Christopher Robin and Pooh could escape by Climbing Trees, and Kanga could escape by Jumping, and Rabbit could escape by Burrowing, and Owl could escape by Flying, and Eeyore could escape by—by Making a Loud Noise Until Rescued, and here am I, surrounded by water and I can't do *anything*."

It went on raining and raining. Every day the water got a little higher, until it nearly reached Piglet's window...and still he hadn't done *anything*.

"I wonder what Christopher Robin would do?" he thought to himself.

Then suddenly he remembered a story Christopher Robin had told him. It was about a man on a desert island who wrote something in a bottle and threw it into the sea. Piglet thought that if he wrote something in a bottle and threw it in the water, perhaps somebody would come and rescue *him*!

He left the window and began to search his house. At last he found a pencil, a small piece of dry paper, and a bottle. He wrote on one side of the paper:

HELP!
PIGLIT (ME)

and on the other side:

IT'S ME PIGLIT, HELP HELP!

Then he put the paper in the bottle, and he closed the bottle as tightly as he could. Piglet threw the bottle out of his window, as far as he could throw—*splash!*—and soon it was floating away. When Piglet couldn't see the bottle anymore, he knew that he had done all that he could to save himself.

"So now," he thought, "somebody else will have to do something. I hope they will do it soon." And then he gave a long sigh and said, "I wish Pooh were here."

* * *

When the rain began Pooh was asleep. It rained, and it rained, and it rained, and he slept and he slept and he slept. He had had a tiring day. Remember how he discovered the North Pole? Well, he was so proud of himself that he asked Christopher Robin if there were any other Poles to be discovered.

"There's a South Pole," said Christopher Robin, "and I think there's an East Pole and a West Pole, though people don't like talking about them."

Pooh was excited when he heard this, and wanted to have an Expotition to discover the East Pole. But Christopher Robin had plans with Kanga, so Pooh went out to discover the East Pole by himself. I don't remember whether he discovered it or not, but he was so tired when he got home that he fell asleep in his chair in the middle of supper.

He dreamed that he was at the East Pole. It was a very cold pole full of snow and ice. He was sleeping in a beehive, but there was no room for his legs, so he had left them outside. Then Wild Woozles came and ate all the fur off his legs. The more they ate, the colder his legs got, until suddenly he woke up saying *Ow!*—and there he was, sitting in his chair with his feet in the water, and water all round him!

He splashed to his door and looked out...

"This is Serious," said Pooh. "I must Escape."

So he took his largest pot of honey and escaped with it to a wide branch of his tree, high above the water. Then he climbed down again and escaped with another pot...and when he had finished Escaping, Pooh was sitting on his branch with ten pots of honey...

Two days later, Pooh was sitting on his branch with four pots of honey...

Three days later, Pooh was sitting on his branch with one pot of honey.

Four days later, Pooh was sitting on his branch alone...

And that morning, Piglet's bottle floated past him. Pooh cried "Honey!" and jumped into the water. He took the bottle, and struggled back to his tree.

"Bother!" said Pooh, as he opened it. "There is nothing here. What's this paper?"

He took it out and looked at it.

"It's a Missage," he said, "That letter is a 'P,' and 'P' means 'Pooh,' so it's a very important Missage for me. But I can't read it. I must find

Surrounded by Water

a Clever Reader like Christopher Robin or Owl or Piglet, and they will tell me what this missage means. Only I can't swim. Bother!"

Then he had an idea. I think that for a Bear of Very Little Brain, it was a good idea. He said to himself:

"If a bottle can float, then a jar can float. If it's a big enough jar, then I can sit on top of it."

So he took his biggest jar and closed it tight.

"All boats need a name," he said, "so I shall call mine *The Floating Bear*." He dropped his boat into the water and jumped in after it.

After struggling with *The Floating Bear* for a while, Pooh finally lay on top of it, and paddled quickly with his feet.

Christopher Robin lived at the very top of the Forest. It rained, and it rained, and it rained, and so most of the time he stayed indoors. But

every morning he went out with his umbrella to put a stick in the place where the water came up to, and every next morning he went out and couldn't see his stick any more. So he put another stick in the place where the water came up to, and then he walked home again. Each morning he had a shorter walk than the morning before. On the morning of the fifth day he saw water all round him. For the first time in his life, he felt that he was on a real island. It was very exciting.

It was on this morning that Owl flew over to say "How do you do?" to his friend Christopher Robin.

SURROUNDED BY WATER

"I say, Owl," said Christopher Robin, "isn't this fun? I'm on an island!"

"The atmospheric conditions have been very unfavorable lately," said Owl.

"The what?"

"It has been raining," explained Owl.

"Yes," said Christopher Robin. "It has."

"However, the prospects are rapidly becoming more favorable. At any moment—"

"Have you seen Pooh?"

"No. At any moment—"

"I hope he's all right," said Christopher Robin. "I've been wondering about him. I think Piglet's with him. Do you think they're all right, Owl?"

"I expect so. You see, at any moment—"

"Please go and see, Owl. I love Pooh very much, and he might do something silly. Do you see, Owl?"

"Yes," said Owl. "I'll go. I'll be back soon." And he flew off.

In a little while he returned.

"Pooh isn't there," he said.

"Not there?"

"He *was* there. He *was* sitting on a branch

of a tree outside his house with nine pots of honey. But he isn't there now."

"Oh, Pooh!" cried Christopher Robin. "Where *are* you?"

"Here I am," said a voice behind him.

"Pooh!"

They ran to each other and hugged.

"How did you get here, Pooh?" asked Christopher Robin.

"On my boat," said Pooh proudly. "I found a Very Important Missage in a bottle, and because I have water in my eyes, I couldn't read it. So I brought it to you. On my boat."

With these proud words he gave Christopher Robin the missage.

"But it's from Piglet!" cried Christopher Robin when he read it. "We must rescue him at once! I thought he was with *you*, Pooh. Owl, could you rescue him on your back?"

"I don't think so," said Owl. "It is doubtful if the necessary dorsal muscles—"

"Then would you fly to him at *once* and say that Rescue is Coming? And Pooh and I will think of a Rescue and come as quick as we can." And so Owl flew off.

"Now then, Pooh," said Christopher Robin, "where's your boat?"

"There!" Pooh pointed proudly to *The Floating Bear.*

It wasn't what Christopher Robin expected. The more he looked at it, the more he thought what a Brave and Clever Bear Pooh was.

"But it's too small for the two of us," said Christopher Robin sadly.

"Three of us with Piglet."

"That makes it even smaller. Oh, Pooh Bear, what do we do?"

And then this Bear, Pooh Bear, Winnie-the-Pooh, F.O.P. (Friend of Piglet's), R.C. (Rabbit's Companion), P.D. (Pole Discoverer), E.C. and T.F. (Eeyore's Comforter and Tail-finder)—in fact, Pooh himself—said something so clever that Christopher Robin could only look at him with mouth open and eyes staring. He wondered if this was really the Bear of Very Little Brain that he knew and loved.

"We might go in your umbrella," said Pooh.

"?"

"We might go in your umbrella," said Pooh.

"??"

"We might go in your umbrella," said Pooh.

"!!!!!!"

For suddenly Christopher Robin saw that they might. He opened his umbrella and put its point downwards in the water. It floated but wobbled. When they both got in together, it wobbled no longer.

"I shall call this boat *The Brain of Pooh*,"

said Christopher Robin, and *The Brain of Pooh* sailed off.

Later, Piglet might say that he had been in Very Great Danger but he was only in danger when Owl arrived and began telling a very long story.

It was about Owl's aunt who had once laid a seagull's egg by mistake, and the story went on and on, just like this sentence, until Piglet, who was listening out of his window, fell asleep and slipped slowly out of the window towards the water, when luckily, a sudden loud noise from Owl woke Piglet and gave him time to save himself and say, "How interesting!" when at last he saw the ship, *Brain of Pooh* (*Captain*, C. Robin; *1st Mate*, P. Bear) coming over to rescue him...

And as that is the end of the story, and I am very tired after that last sentence, I think I shall stop there.

CHAPTER TEN

In which Christopher Robin gives a Pooh Party, and we say good-bye

One day when the sun had returned to the Forest in the month of May, Christopher Robin whistled in his special way, and Owl came flying to see what he wanted.

"Owl," said Christopher Robin, "I am going to give a party."

"You are, are you?" said Owl.

"It's a special party. It's for Pooh, because of what he did when he saved Piglet from the flood."

"Oh, that's what it's for, is it?" said Owl.

"Yes, so please tell Pooh as quickly as you can, and all the others, because it will be tomorrow."

"Oh, it will, will it?" said Owl, being as helpful as possible.

We Say Good-Bye

"So will you go and tell them, Owl?"

Owl tried to think of something wise to say, but couldn't, so he flew off to tell the others. The first person he told was Pooh.

"Pooh," he said. "Christopher Robin is giving a party."

"Oh!" said Pooh. Seeing that Owl wanted him to say something else, he said, "Will there be cakes with pink sugar icing?"

Owl didn't want to talk about cakes with pink sugar icing so he told Pooh what Christopher Robin had said exactly. Then he flew off to Eeyore.

"A party for Me?" thought Pooh. "How wonderful!" He wondered if all the other animals knew that it was a special Pooh Party, and if Christopher Robin had told them about *The Floating Bear* and *The Brain of Pooh*. He thought it would be awful if nobody knew what the party was for. The more he thought about it, the more worried he became. And his worry turned into a song. It was an

ANXIOUS POOH SONG

3 Cheers for Pooh!
(*For Who?*)
For Pooh—
(*Why what did he do?*)
I thought you knew;
He saved his friend from a wetting!
3 Cheers for Bear!
(*For where?*)
For Bear—
He couldn't swim,
But he rescued him!
(*He rescued who?*)
Oh, listen, do!
I am talking of Pooh—
(*Of who?*)
Of Pooh!
(*I'm sorry I keep forgetting.*)
Well, Pooh was a Bear of Enormous Brain—
(*Just say it again!*)
Of enormous brain—
(*Of enormous what?*)

Well, he ate a lot,
And I don't know if he could swim or not,
But he managed to float
On a sort of boat
(*On a sort of what?*)
Well, a sort of pot—
So now let's give him three hearty cheers
(*So now let's give him three hearty whiches!*)
And hope he'll be with us for years and years,
And grow in health and wisdom and riches!
3 Cheers for Pooh!
(*For who?*)
For Pooh—
3 Cheers for Bear!
(*For where?*)
For Bear—
3 Cheers for the wonderful Winnie-the-Pooh!
(*Just tell me, somebody—WHAT DID HE DO?*)

While this was going on inside Pooh, Owl was talking to Eeyore.

"Eeyore," said Owl, "Christopher Robin is giving a party."

"Interesting," said Eeyore. "I suppose they will send me things that have been thrown away.

How Kind and Thoughtful."

"There is an Invitation for you."

"What's that?"

"An Invitation!"

Eeyore shook his head.

"You mean Piglet. The little one. That's Piglet. I'll tell him."

"No, no!" said Owl, getting quite cross. "Christopher Robin said 'All of them! Tell all of them.'"

"All of them, except Eeyore?"

"All of them," said Owl.

"Ah!" said Eeyore. "A mistake, of course. But I will come. Just don't blame *me* if it rains."

But it didn't rain. Christopher Robin had made a long table out of wood, and they all sat round it. Christopher Robin sat at one end, and Pooh sat at the other. In between them sat Owl,

Eeyore, and Piglet on one side and Rabbit, Roo, and Kanga on the other.

Rabbit's friends and family sat on the grass, waiting and hoping that somebody would speak to them.

It was Roo's first party and he was very excited. As soon as they sat down he began to talk.

"Hallo, Pooh!" he squeaked.

"Hallo, Roo!" said Pooh.

Roo jumped up and down in his seat and then began again.

"Hallo, Eeyore!" said Roo.

Eeyore nodded gloomily at him. "It will rain soon, see if it doesn't," he said.

Roo looked, and it didn't rain, so he said "Hallo, Owl!"—and Owl said "Hallo, my little fellow," in a kindly way.

Kanga said to Roo, "Drink your milk first, dear, and talk afterwards."

Roo, who was drinking his milk, tried to say that he could do both at once...and then he had to be patted on the back and dried for quite some time afterwards.

When they finished eating, Christopher Robin banged on the table with his spoon.

We Say Good-Bye

Everybody stopped talking, except Roo, who was hiccuping.

"This party," said Christopher Robin, "is a party because of what someone did, and we all know who it was. It's his party, and I've got a present for him. Here it is." Then he looked

round and whispered, "Where is it?"

While he was looking, Eeyore cleared his throat and began to speak.

"Friends," he said, "I am happy to see you all at my party. What I did was nothing. Any of you—except Rabbit and Owl and Kanga—would have done the same. Oh, and Pooh. Piglet and Roo couldn't do anything because they are too small. I did not do it for a present but because I wanted to help. I feel that we should all—"

"What's Eeyore talking about?" Piglet whispered to Pooh.

"I don't know," said Pooh sadly.

"I thought this was *your* party."

"I thought so *too*. But I suppose it isn't."

"I'd prefer if it was yours rather than Eeyore's," said Piglet.

"So would I," said Pooh.

"AS—I—WAS—SAYING," said Eeyore loudly and sternly, "I feel that—"

"Here it is!" cried Christopher Robin excitedly. "Pass it down—it's for silly old Pooh."

"For Pooh?" said Eeyore.

We Say Good-Bye

"Of course it is. The best bear in all the world."

"I might have known," said Eeyore. "I can't complain. I have my friends. And somebody spoke to me yesterday."

Nobody was listening for they were all saying, "Open it, Pooh," "What is it, Pooh?" "I know what it is," "No, you don't," and other helpful comments. Pooh opened it as quickly as he could.

When Pooh saw what it was, he nearly fell down, he was so pleased. It was a Special Pencil Case. There were pencils marked "B" for Bear, "HB" for Helping Bear, and "BB" for Brave Bear. There was a knife for sharpening the pencils, and indiarubber for rubbing out anything you spelt wrong. There was a ruler for ruling lines, and inches marked on the ruler in case you wanted to know how many inches anything was. There were Blue Pencils, Red Pencils, and Green Pencils for saying special things. And they were all for Pooh.

"Oh!" said Pooh. "Thank-you."

When they had all said "Good-bye" and "Thank-you" to Christopher Robin, Pooh and Piglet walked home together in the sunset. For a long time they were silent.

"When you wake up in the morning, Pooh," said Piglet at last, "what's the first thing you say to yourself?"

WE SAY GOOD-BYE

"What's for breakfast?" said Pooh. "What do *you* say, Piglet?"

"I say, I wonder what exciting thing will happen *today*?" said Piglet.

Pooh nodded thoughtfully.

"It's the same thing," he said.

* * *

"And what happened?" asked Christopher Robin.

"When?"

"Next morning."

"I don't know."

"Could you think, and tell me and Pooh sometime?"

"If you wanted it very much."

"Pooh does," said Christopher Robin.

Christopher Robin sighed deeply, picked his bear up by the leg and walked toward the door. Then he turned and said, "Coming to see me have my bath?"

"Maybe," I said.

"Was Pooh's pencil case better than mine?"

"It was just the same," I said.

He nodded and went out...and in a moment I heard Winnie-the-Pooh—*bump, bump, bump*—going up the stairs behind him.

Word List

・本文で使われている全ての語を掲載しています（LEVEL 1、2）。ただし、LEVEL 3 以上は、中学校レベルの語を含みません。

・語形が規則変化する語の見出しは原形で示しています。不規則変化語は本文中で使われている形になっています。

・一般的な意味を紹介していますので、一部の語で本文で実際に使われている品詞や意味と合っていないことがあります。

・品詞は以下のように示しています。

名 名詞	代 代名詞	形 形容詞	副 副詞	動 動詞	助 助動詞
前 前置詞	接 接続詞	間 間投詞	冠 冠詞	略 略語	俗 俗語
頭 接頭語	尾 接尾語	号 記号	関 関係代名詞		

A

- **a ～ or two** 1～か2～、2、3の
- **about to** 《be －》まさに～しようとしている、～するところだ
- **accidentally** 副 偶然に
- **acorn** 名 ドングリ
- **acre** 名 エーカー《面積の単位。約4,046.7平方メートル》
- **actually** 副 実は
- **add** 動 言い添える
- **admire** 動 ～を称賛する
- **adventure** 名 冒険
- **after that** その後
- **afterwards** 副 その後、のちに
- **ah** 間《驚き・悲しみ・賞賛などを表して》ああ、やっぱり
- **aha** 間 はは！、へへん！、わかった
- **Alexander Beetle** アレクサンダー・ビートル《名前》
- **all** 熟 all over ～中で、全体に亘って、～の至る所で all right 大丈夫で、よろしい、申し分ない、わかった。承知した all round 全体的に、当たり一面に、四方に all the way down 端から端まで all the way to ～までずっと not at all 少しも～でない、全くそん

なことはない
- **ambush** 名 待ち伏せ
- **and so** そこで、それだから、それで
- **anxious** 形 心配な、不安な
- **anxiously** 副 心配して
- **any** 熟 not ～ any more もう［これ以上］～ない
- **anybody** 代 ①《疑問文・条件節で》誰か ②《否定文で》誰も（～ない）③《肯定文で》誰でも anybody who ～する人はだれでも
- **anyhow** 副 いずれにせよ、ともかく
- **anymore** 副《通例否定文、疑問文で》今はもう、これ以上
- **anyone** 代 ①《疑問文・条件節で》誰か ②《否定文で》誰も（～ない）
- **appear** 動 現れる、姿を見せる
- **argue** 動 言い争う
- **arrive at** ～に着く
- **as** 熟 as if あたかも～のように、まるで～みたいに as long as ～である限りは as soon as ～するとすぐ、～するや否や as ～ as one can できる限り～ as ～ as possible できるだけ～

150

WORD LIST

- **ashamed** 形 恥ずかしい
- **ask ~ if** ~かどうか尋ねる
- **asleep** 形 眠って（いる状態の）副 眠って **fall asleep** 眠り込む, 寝入る
- **atmospheric** 形 大気の
- **attached to** ~にくっついている
- **awful** 形 ①ひどい, 不愉快な ②恐ろしい
- **awoke** 動 awake（目覚めさせる）の過去

B

- **back** 熟 **come back** 戻る **get back to** ~に戻る **go back to** ~に帰る［戻る］**put ~ back** ~を（もとの場所に）戻す, 返す
- **backwards** 副 後方へ, 後ろ向きに
- **balloon** 名 風船
- **bang** 名 衝撃音, バンという音 動 強く打つ
- **bar** 名 棒
- **bath** 熟 **have a cold bath** 冷水風呂に入る
- **bath-water** 名 お風呂の湯, 水
- **bear** 名 クマ 動 我慢する
- **because of** ~のために, ~の理由で
- **bed** 熟 **go to bed** 床につく, 寝る
- **bedtime** 名 就寝の時刻
- **bee** 名 ミツバチ **queen bee** 女王バチ
- **beech-tree** 名 ブナの木
- **beehive** 名 ミツバチの巣箱
- **behind** 前 ①~の後ろに, ~の背後に ②~に遅れて 副 後ろに, 後に **leave behind** ~を忘れてくる
- **bell-rope** 名 呼び鈴のひも
- **below** 前 ~より下に 副 下に［へ］

- **bend over** ~に身をかがめる
- **bent** 動 bend（曲がる）の過去, 過去分詞
- **bit of** 《a–》少しの~
- **blame** 動 とがめる, 非難する
- **blow** 動 ①（風が）吹く, （風が）~を吹き飛ばす ②息を吹く **blow off** 吹き飛ぶ［飛ばす］**blow up**（風船などが）ふくらむ, 破裂する［させる］
- **blown** 動 blow（吹く）の過去分詞
- **board** 名 板, 掲示板
- **bonhommy** 形 温容な, 純朴な《フランス語》
- **bon-hommy** 形 温容な, 純朴な《フランス語》
- **boot** 名 《-s》長靴, ブーツ
- **bother** 間 まったくもう, いやだなあ 動 困る, 困らせる, 悩ませる
- **bottom** 名 底, 下部
- **brain** 名 ①脳 ②知力
- **branch** 名 枝
- **brave** 形 勇敢な
- **bravely** 副 勇敢に（も）
- **break down** 泣き出す
- **breath** 名 息, 呼吸 **shortness of breath** 息切れ
- **breathe** 動 呼吸する
- **brighten up**（顔などが）輝く
- **bring home** 家に持ってくる
- **brush away** 払い落とす
- **bthuthdth** 名 birthday（誕生日）のつづり間違い
- **bthuthdy** 名 birthday（誕生日）のつづり間違い
- **bump** 名 ドン, ガタン《ぶつかる音》
- **burrow** 動 穴を掘る
- **burst** 動 破裂させる
- **bush** 名 茂み
- **but** 熟 **not ~ but** ~ではなくて…

WINNIE-THE-POOH

- **buzz** 名 ブンブン（という音）
- **buzzing-noise** 名 ブーンという音
- **by oneself** 一人で，自分だけで
- **by this time** もうすでに

C

- **call** 熟 call down 下に向かって叫ぶ　call in ～を呼ぶ　call out 叫ぶ，呼び出す，声を掛ける　call someone by a name （人）を名前で呼ぶ　call to ～に声をかける
- **can** 熟 Can I ～? ～してもよいですか。Can you ～? ～してくれますか。as ～ as one can できる限り～　can hardly とても～できない
- **candle** 名 ろうそく
- **captain** 名 船長
- **capture** 動 捕える
- **case** 熟 in case ～だといけないので，念のため，万が一の～に備えて
- **caught** 動 catch（捕まえる）の過去・過去分詞　get caught 捕らえられる
- **chapter** 名 （書物の）章
- **charming** 形 魅力的な
- **check** 動 確認する
- **cheer** 動 ～を元気付ける，～に喝采を送る　名 《-s》乾杯　cheers for ～に乾杯　cheer ～ up ～を元気づける
- **cheerfully** 副 陽気に，快活に
- **cheese** 名 チーズ
- **chestnut** 名 栗の木，トチの木
- **Christopher Robin** クリストファー・ロビン《人名》
- **circle** 熟 in a circle 円形に
- **clear** 形 はっきりした，明白な　動 ①すっきりさせる ②晴れる　clear up （空が）晴れる
- **clever** 形 頭のよい，利口な

- **climb out** 抜け出す
- **close to** 《be –》～に近い
- **cnoke** 動 knock（ノックする）のつづり間違い
- **cold** 熟 have a cold bath 冷水風呂に入る
- **color** 名 色 動 ～に色をつける
- **colored** 形 色のついた
- **come** 熟 come and ～しに行く　come around ぶらっと訪れる　come back 戻る come down 下へ降りる，下りて来る come in 中に入る，（命令形で）お入りください come into ～に入ってくる come off 取れる，はずれる come on ①おいで，いいかげんにしろ，もうよせ ②～に行く come out 出てくる，外へ出る come over to ～にやって来る come up to ～のそばまでやってくる
- **comfort** 動 ～を慰める，安心させる
- **comforter** 名 慰める人
- **comforting** 形 気分が安らぐ
- **comfortingly** 副 励ますように
- **comment** 名 意見，コメント
- **companion** 名 仲間
- **complain** 動 不平[苦情]を言う
- **condensed** 形 濃縮された
- **condition** 名 状態，様相
- **confused** 形 困惑した，混乱した
- **'cos** 略 《= because》なぜなら，～ので
- **cottleston pie** カトルストン・パイ《ベーコンと卵のパイ》
- **cough** 名 せき，せき払い
- **could** 熟 Could you please ～? ～していただけないのでしょうか。Could you ～? ～してくださいますか。If +《主語》+ could ～できればなあ《仮定法》
- **count** 動 数える
- **course** 熟 of course もちろん，当

152

WORD LIST

然
- **cover** 名 覆い, カバー
- **crack** 名 ピシッ《ひびが入って割れる音》
- **crash** 動 衝突する 名 衝突(音), 破壊
- **crawl** 動 はう, 腹ばいで進む
- **crossly** 副 不機嫌に, すねて
- **crustimoney** 形 customary (慣習的)の言い[聞き]間違い
- **cunning** 形 巧妙な
- **cupboard** 名 食器棚, 戸棚
- **customary** 形 慣習的な

D

- **dandelion** 名 タンポポ
- **danger** 熟 out of danger 危機を脱して
- **day** 熟 every day 毎日 one day ある日
- **dearie** 名 あなた, 親愛なる人
- **decide to do** ～することに決める
- **deeply** 副 深く
- **definitely** 副 明確に, 確実に
- **desert** 形 無人の
- **despair** 名 絶望
- **dicsovered** 動 discovered (発見された)のつづり間違い
- **dig** 動 掘る
- **disappointed** 形 がっかりした
- **discoverer** 名 発見者
- **ditch** 名 水路, 溝
- **do** 熟 How do you do? こんにちは。
- **donkey** 名 ロバ
- **dorsal** 形 背面の
- **doubtful** 形 不確かな
- **down** 熟 down there 下の方で up and down 行ったり来たり, あちこちと

- **downstairs** 副 階下へ
- **downwards** 副 下方へ
- **dreamily** 副 うっとりと
- **drift** 動 漂う

E

- **each other** お互いに
- **earnestly** 副 まじめに
- **edge** 名 端, 縁
- **Edward Bear** エドワード・ベア《名前》
- **Eeyore** 名 イーヨー《名前》
- **either A or B** Aかそれともり B
- **end** 熟 at the end of ～の終わりに
- **enjoy oneself** 楽しく過ごす
- **enormous** 形 非常に大きい, ばく大な
- **entirely** 副 完全に, まったく
- **er** 間 ああ, あのう, ええと
- **escape** 動 逃げる, (危険などから)免れる
- **even if** たとえ～でも
- **every day** 毎日
- **every time** ～するときはいつも
- **everybody** 代 誰でも, 皆
- **everything** 代 すべてのこと[もの], 何もかも
- **example** 熟 for example たとえば
- **except** 前 ～を除いて, ～のほかは 接 ～ということを除いて
- **excited** 形 興奮した, わくわくした
- **excitedly** 副 興奮して
- **exciting** 形 興奮させる, わくわくさせる
- **exercise** 名 運動, 体操

153

WINNIE-THE-POOH

- □ **expect** 動 予期［予測］する，(当然のこととして) 期待する
- □ **expedition** 名 探検，遠征［探検］隊
- □ **expotition** 名 expedition (探検) の言い［聞き］間違い

F

- □ **face** 熟 fall on one's face うつ伏せに倒れる
- □ **fact** 熟 in fact つまり，要するに
- □ **fall** 熟 fall asleep 眠り込む，寝入る fall down 転ぶ fall off 落ちる fall on one's face うつ伏せに倒れる fall over backward 後ろに倒れる
- □ **fallen** 動 fall (落ちる) の過去分詞
- □ **far** 熟 far away 遠く離れて far from ～から遠い from far away 遠くから so far ある程度
- □ **farther** 副 (距離的に) さらに，もっと
- □ **favorable** 形 好都合な，さい先の明るい
- □ **feeling** 名 感じ，気持ち sinking feeling 虚脱感，気がめいる感じ
- □ **fellow** 名 仲間，同士
- □ **fetch** 動 行って連れてくる
- □ **fierce** 形 どう猛な，残忍な
- □ **fill up** (穴・すき間を) いっぱいに満たす
- □ **find one's way** たどり着く
- □ **finish doing** ～するのを終える
- □ **firm** 形 断固とした
- □ **first** 熟 at first 最初は，初めのうちは for the first time in one's life 生まれて初めて
- □ **firstly** 副 初めに，まず第一に
- □ **fit** 動 合致［適合］する (大きさや形が～) に合う
- □ **float** 動 ①浮く，浮かぶ ②漂流する

float away 流れていく float up into the sky 空に浮かんでいく
- □ **flood** 名 洪水
- □ **fly off** 飛び去る
- □ **fly over** 上空を飛ぶ
- □ **fly to** ～まで飛んで行く
- □ **follow** 熟 as follows 次の通りで
- □ **fond of** 《be－》～が大好きだ．～を好む
- □ **foolish** 形 おろかな，ばかばかしい
- □ **forget to do** ～することを忘れる
- □ **forward** 副 前方に
- □ **freeze** 動 底冷えする
- □ **French** 形 フランス (語) の
- □ **friendly** 形 友情のこもった
- □ **fright** 名 恐怖，激しい驚き
- □ **frighten** 動 驚かせる，びっくりさせる
- □ **full of** ～で一杯の
- □ **full-up** 形 いっぱいに詰まった
- □ **funny** 形 ①おもしろい ②奇妙な，おかしい
- □ **fur** 名 毛，毛皮

G

- □ **gaze** 動 凝視する
- □ **general** 形 一般の，普通の
- □ **get** 熟 get ～ across ～を向こう側へ渡らせる get back to ～に戻る get caught 捕らえられる get home 家に着く［帰る］ get in 中に入る，入り込む，乗り込む get into ～に入る get near 接近する get ～ on ～を着る，はく get out 外に出る get ready 用意［支度］をする get thin やせる get to ～に達する［到着する］ get up 起き上がる，立ち上がる
- □ **gloomily** 副 陰気に
- □ **gloomy** 形 憂うつな

154

WORD LIST

- [ ] **go** 熟 go after ～を追い求める go and ～しに行く go around 一回りする，周りを回る go away 立ち去る go back to ～に帰る[戻る] go doing ～をしに行く go for a walk 散歩に行く go home 帰宅する go in 中に入る go off 出かける，出発する go on 続く，続ける，起こる go on and on 延々としゃべる，どんどん続ける go on with ～を続ける go out 外出する，外へ出る go over ～へ渡る go to bed 床につく，寝る go up ～に上がる，登る let go 手を放す let go of ～から手を離す off someone go（人）が出かけていく there you go ほらね

- [ ] **goloptious** 形 voluptuous（こってりとした）の言い［聞き］間違い

- [ ] **good at** 《be –》～が得意だ

- [ ] **good-bye** 間 さようなら 名 別れのあいさつ

- [ ] **gorse-bush** 名 ハリエニシダの茂み

- [ ] **grand** 形 立派な，ぜいたくな

- [ ] **grass** 名 草，芝生

- [ ] **grey** 形 灰色の

- [ ] **ground** 熟 on the ground 地面に

- [ ] **growly** 形 うなり声のような

- [ ] **gun** 名 銃

H

- [ ] **ha** 間 ほう，は《驚き・喜び・笑い声などを表す》

- [ ] **hail** 名 ひょう，あられ

- [ ] **halfway through** 道の半ばで

- [ ] **hallo** 間 こんにちは，やあ

- [ ] **halt** 動 止まる，停止する

- [ ] **hand in hand** 手をとり合って

- [ ] **handkerchief** 名 ハンカチ

- [ ] **hang** 動 かける，ぶら下がる

- [ ] **happily** 副 幸福に，楽しく

- [ ] **happiness** 名 幸せ，喜び

- [ ] **happy to do** 《be –》～してうれしい，喜んで～する

- [ ] **hard** 熟 hard to ～し難い try hard to ～に尽力する

- [ ] **hardly** 副 ほとんど～でない can hardly とても～できない

- [ ] **have** 熟 don't have to ～する必要はない have a cold bath 冷水風呂に入る have a headache 頭痛がする

- [ ] **haycorn** 名 acorn（ドングリ）の言い［聞き］間違い

- [ ] **head** 熟 put one's head down 頭を下げる

- [ ] **headache** 名 頭痛 have a headache 頭痛がする

- [ ] **heart** 熟 know ～ by heart ～を暗記している

- [ ] **hearty** 形 心のこもった

- [ ] **heather** 名 ヒース《荒野にはえる植物》

- [ ] **Heffalump** 名 ヘッファランプ《ゾウに似た空想上の動物》

- [ ] **heffalumping** 形 ヘッファランプっぽい

- [ ] **hellible** 形 terrible（恐ろしい）の言い間違い

- [ ] **helpful** 形 役に立つ，参考になる

- [ ] **helping** 形 救いの，助けの

- [ ] **Henry Pootel** ヘンリー・プーテル《名前》

- [ ] **here** 熟 Here it is. はい，どうぞ。I wish ～ were here ～がここにいればいいのになあ。《仮定法過去》here is ～ こちらは～です。

- [ ] **herrible** 形 terrible（恐ろしい）の言い間違い

- [ ] **hey** 間 ヘイ，ほら，おい

- [ ] **hiccup** 動 しゃっくりする

- [ ] **hid** 動 hide（隠す）の過去，過去分詞

- [ ] **hide** 動 隠す

- [ ] **hipy** 形 happy（幸せな）のつづり間

155

Winnie-the-Pooh

違い

- □ **ho** 間《驚き・喜びなどを表して》ほお，ほー
- □ **hoar-frost** 名霜
- □ **hoffalump** 名heffalump（ヘッファランプ）の言い間違い
- □ **hold on tight to** ～をしっかりつかむ
- □ **hold on to** ～にしがみつく
- □ **hold up** ～を持ち上げる
- □ **home** 熟at home 自宅で bring home 家に持ってくる get home 家に着く［帰る］go home 帰宅する take someone home ～を家に持ち帰る
- □ **honeycomb** 名ハチの巣
- □ **honey-jar** 名ハチミツのつぼ
- □ **hoof** 名ひづめ
- □ **hooray** 間フレー，万歳
- □ **hopeful** 形希望に満ちた
- □ **hopefully** 副希望を持って
- □ **horralump** 名heffalump（ヘッファランプ）の言い間違い
- □ **horrible** 形恐ろしい
- □ **hostile** 形敵意をもった，敵の
- □ **how** 熟how are you? ごきげんよう。how do you do? こんにちは。how's things? ごけんいかが。 how to どのように～したらいいか
- □ **however** 接けれども，だが
- □ **hug** 動しっかりと抱き締める
- □ **huge** 形巨大な
- □ **hullo** 間やあ，ハロー
- □ **hum** 動鼻歌を歌う 名鼻歌
- □ **Hundred Acre Wood** 100エーカーの森
- □ **hung** 動hang（かかる）の過去，過去分詞
- □ **hunny** 名honey（ハチミツ）のつづり間違い
- □ **hunting** 名狩り，捜索

- □ **hush** 間しっ！，静かに！

I

- □ **icing** 名砂糖衣
- □ **if** 熟If +《主語》+ could ～できればなあ《仮定法》as if あたかも～のように，まるで～みたいに ask ～ if ～かどうか尋ねる even if たとえ～でも if only ～でありさえすれば if possible 可能なら see if ～かどうかを確かめる what if もし～だったらどうなるだろうか wonder if ～ではないかと思う
- □ **imagine** 動想像する，心に思い描く
- □ **imitate** 動まねる
- □ **immersion** 名浸水
- □ **impress** 動感動させる
- □ **in turns** 代わる代わる
- □ **in which** 略the chapter［story］in which の略
- □ **in you go** 中に入って
- □ **inch** 名インチ《長さの単位。1/12フィート，2.54cm》
- □ **indeed** 副実際，本当に
- □ **indiarubber** 名消しゴム
- □ **indoors** 副室内で，屋内で
- □ **instead** 副その代わりに instead of ～の代わりに，～ではなく
- □ **intent** 名意図
- □ **invitation** 名招待状
- □ **issue** 動公表する
- □ **itself** 代それ自身

J

- □ **jam** 名ジャム
- □ **jar** 名（広口の）瓶，壺
- □ **jaw** 名あご

156

WORD LIST

- **jigget** 動跳ね回る
- **joke** 名冗談，ジョーク **play a joke** 悪ふざけをする
- **journey** 名（遠い目的地への）旅
- **jump** 熟 **jump into** ～に飛び込む **jump out at** ～の前に躍り出る **jump out of** ～から飛び出す **jump up and down** 飛び跳ねる
- **just as** とたんに，～するや否や

K

- **Kanga** 名カンガ《名前》
- **kindly** 形親切な，思いやりのある 副親切に，優しく
- **knife** 名ナイフ，小刀
- **knock** 動ノックする，たたく 名戸をたたくこと［音］
- **knocker** 名ドアノッカー
- **know** 熟 **know ～ by heart** ～を暗記している **never know** ～のことはわからない，知るよしもない

L

- **label** 名標札，ラベル
- **laid** 動lay（産卵する）の過去，過去分詞
- **lap** 名ひざ
- **larch-tree** 名カラマツ
- **last** 熟 **at last** ついに，とうとう，最後に
- **lately** 副近ごろ，最近
- **laugh to oneself** 忍び笑いする
- **lay** 動①置く ②卵を産む ③lie（横たわる）の過去
- **lean** 動もたれる，寄りかかる
- **least** 名最小，最少 **at least** 少なくとも
- **leave behind** ～を忘れてくる

- **let** 熟 **Let me see.** ええと。 **let go** 手を放す **let go of** ～から手を離す **let us** どうか私たちに～させてください
- **lick** 動なめる，なめて食べる 名なめること
- **lie** 動横たわる，寝る
- **life** 熟 **for the first time in one's life** 生まれて初めて
- **lift** 動持ち上げる，上がる
- **like** 熟 **Would you like ～?** ～はいかがですか。 **like this** このような，こんなふうに **look like** ～のように見える，～のようだ **sound like** ～のように聞こえる **would like to** ～したいと思う
- **listening-to-me-humming** 名私のハミングを聞いてくれる（人物）
- **long** 熟 **as long as** ～である限りは
- **longer** 熟 **no longer** もはや～でない［～しない］
- **look** 熟 **look after** ～の後を見送る **look around** まわりを見回す **look around for** ～を捜し求める **look down** 見下ろす，下を見る **look for** ～を探す **look in** 中を見る **look into** ～の中を見る **look like** ～のように見える，～のようだ **look out** 外を見る **look up** 見上げる，調べる **take a look at** ～をちょっと見る
- **lot of** 《a－》たくさんの～
- **loudly** 副大声で，騒がしく
- **lovely** 形すばらしい
- **loving** 形愛情のこもった
- **lovingly** 副愛情を込めて
- **luckily** 副運よく，幸いにも
- **lump** 動のっしのっしと歩く
- **luncheon** 名昼食会

M

- [ ] **make** 熟 make a mistake 間違いをする make noise 音を立てる make sure 確かめる，確認する make up 作り出す，考え出す make ~ out of ~を…から作る
- [ ] **manage** 動 どうにか～する
- [ ] **march through** ～を行進する
- [ ] **mark** 名 跡，へこみ 動 印［記号］をつける
- [ ] **mate** 名 航海士 1st mate 一等航海士
- [ ] **matter** 熟 What's the matter? どうしたんですか。
- [ ] **meant to be** ～のはずである
- [ ] **middle** 名 中間，最中 in the middle of ～の真ん中［最中］に
- [ ] **might** 動《may の過去》①～かもしれない ②～してもよい，～できる might have ～したかもしれない
- [ ] **mind** 動 気にする，いやがる Never mind. 気にするな。
- [ ] **miserable** 形 みじめな，哀れな
- [ ] **missage** 名 message（連絡）の言い間違い
- [ ] **mistake** 熟 by mistake 誤って make a mistake 間違いをする
- [ ] **modestly** 副 謙遜して
- [ ] **mole** 名 モグラ
- [ ] **moment** 名 瞬間，ちょっとの間，(特定の)時 at any moment 今すぐにも at that moment その時に，その瞬間に for a moment 少しの間 in a moment すぐに
- [ ] **more** 熟 more and more ますます no more もう～ない not ~ any more もう［これ以上］～ない the more ~ the more ～すればするほどますます…
- [ ] **mostly** 副 主として，ほとんど
- [ ] **much** 熟 too much 過度の

- [ ] **muddle** 動 ごちゃ混ぜにする
- [ ] **muddy** 形 ぬかるみの
- [ ] **mug** 名 ジョッキ，マグ
- [ ] **mulberry** 名 クワ，マルベリー《植物》
- [ ] **murmur** 動 呟く，ぶつぶつ言う
- [ ] **muscle** 名 筋肉，腕力
- [ ] **mysterious** 形 謎めいた
- [ ] **mysteriously** 副 意味ありげに

N

- [ ] **nail** 動 くぎで打ちつける
- [ ] **name** 熟 call someone by a name（人）を名前で呼ぶ under the name of ～という名で
- [ ] **near** 熟 get near 接近する
- [ ] **nearly** 副 ほとんど，ほぼ，あやうく
- [ ] **necessary** 形 必要な
- [ ] **need to do** ～する必要がある
- [ ] **neither** 代（2者のうち）どちらも～でない
- [ ] **nephew** 名 おい（甥）
- [ ] **nervously** 副 そわそわと，いらいらして
- [ ] **nest** 名 巣
- [ ] **never** 熟 can never tell with ～のことは分からない never know ～のことはわからない，知るよしもない Never mind. 気にするな。
- [ ] **next to** ～のとなりに
- [ ] **no longer** もはや～でない［～しない］
- [ ] **no more** もう～ない
- [ ] **no one** 誰も［一人も］～ない
- [ ] **nobody** 代 誰も［1人も］～ない
- [ ] **nod** 動 うなずく
- [ ] **noise** 名 騒音，物音 make noise 音を立てる

WORD LIST

□ **none** 代 (〜の) 何も [誰も・少しも] …ない

□ **North Pole** 北極

□ **not** 熟 **not at all** 少しも〜でない, 全くそんなことはない **not yet** まだ です **not 〜 any more** もう [これ以上] 〜ない **not 〜 but** 〜ではなくて …

□ **nothing** 熟 **for nothing** むだに

□ **notice** 名 通知, 公告 動 気づく

□ **now** 熟 **for some time now** かなり前から **now that** 今や〜だから

O

□ **oak** 名 オーク《ブナ科の樹木の総称》

□ **of course** もちろん, 当然

□ **off someone go** (人) が出かけていく

□ **old** 形 ①古い, 年をとった ②愛すべき〜ちゃん, 〜のやつ

□ **once** 熟 **at once** すぐに, 同時に **once upon a time** むかしむかし

□ **one** 熟 **no one** 誰も [一人も] 〜ない **one day** ある日 **one of** 〜の1つ [人] **one side** 片側

□ **only** 形 唯一の 副 ただ〜だけ 接 だがしかし **if only** 〜でありさえすれば

□ **oo** 間 ウー

□ **opposite** 形 反対の

□ **or** 熟 **a 〜 or two** 1〜か2〜, 2, 3の

□ **other** 熟 **each other** お互いに

□ **out of** ①〜から外へ, 〜から抜け出して ②〜から作り出して, 〜を材料として ③〜の範囲外に, 〜から離れて **out of danger** 危機を脱して

□ **over** 熟 **all over** 〜中で, 全体に亘って, 〜の至る所で **be over** 終わる **over there** あそこに

□ **ow** 間 ああ！あっ！痛い！

□ **owl** 名 ①オウル《名前》②フクロウ

P

□ **paddle** 動 水を (オールや手などで) かく

□ **papy** 形 happy (幸せな) のつづり間違い

□ **part of** 〜の一部

□ **pass 〜 down** 〜を手渡す

□ **past** 前 〜を過ぎて, 〜を越して

□ **pat** 動 軽くたたく

□ **pathetic** 形 哀れな

□ **pause** 動 思案する, ちょっと止まる

□ **paw** 名 (犬・猫などの) 足, 手

□ **paw-mark** 名 (肉球の) 足あと

□ **perfectly** 副 完全に

□ **perhaps** 副 たぶん, ことによると

□ **pick 〜 out** 〜を拾い出す

□ **pick up** 拾い上げる

□ **Piglet** 名 ピグレット《名前》

□ **Piglit** 名 Piglet (ピグレット) のつづり間違い

□ **pine** 名 マツ (松)

□ **pit** 名 (地面の) 穴, くぼみ

□ **plan to do** 〜を計画する

□ **plate** 名 (浅い) 皿

□ **play a joke** 悪ふざけをする

□ **play with** 〜と一緒に遊ぶ

□ **please** 熟 **Could you please 〜?** 〜していただけないものでしょうか。

□ **pleased** 形 喜んだ

□ **ples** 間 please (なにとぞ) のつづり間違い

□ **plez** 間 please (なにとぞ) のつづり間違い

□ **poetry** 名 詩歌

159

WINNIE-THE-POOH

- □ **pole** 名 ①棒, さお ②極（地）
  North Pole 北極
- □ **politely** 副 礼儀正しく
- □ **pool** 名 水たまり
- □ **pop** 名 パン［ポン］（という音）
- □ **possible** 熟 as 〜 as possible で
  きるだけ 〜 if possible 可能なら
- □ **pot** 名 壺
- □ **prefer** 動（〜のほうが）よいと思う
- □ **prepare for** 〜の準備をする
- □ **pretend** 動 ふりをする, 装う
- □ **private** 形 私的な, 個人の
- □ **procedure** 名 手順
- □ **properly** 副 きっちりと
- □ **proseedcake** 名 procedure（手
  順）の言い［聞き］間違い
- □ **prospect** 名 見込み, 見通し
- □ **pro-thing** 名 プロなんとか
  《provision（食糧）のこと》
- □ **proud** 形 自慢の, 自尊心のある be
  proud of 〜を自慢に思う
- □ **proudly** 副 誇らしげに
- □ **provision** 名 食糧
- □ **pull 〜 out** 〜を引き抜く
- □ **purpose** 熟 on purpose わざと,
  故意に
- □ **push against** 〜を押す
- □ **push one's way through** か
  き分けて進む
- □ **push 〜 forward** 〜を突き出す
- □ **put** 熟 put in 〜の中に入れる put
  on ①〜を身につける, 着る ②〜を…
  の上に置く put one's head down
  頭を下げる put up ①〜を上げる ②
  掲示する put 〜 back 〜を（もとの
  場所に）戻す, 返す put 〜 into 〜を
  …に突っ込む
- □ **puzzle** 動 困惑する, まごつく

Q

- □ **quarter to** 〜時15分前
- □ **queen bee** 女王バチ
- □ **quickly** 副 敏速に, 急いで
- □ **quietly** 副 静かに, 平穏に
- □ **quite** 熟 for quite some time か
  なり長い間

R

- □ **rabbit** 名 ①ラビット《名前》②ウ
  サギ
- □ **rag** 名 ぼろ切れ, 布きれ
- □ **rang** 動 ring（鳴らす）の過去
- □ **rapidly** 副 急速に
- □ **rarely** 副 めったに〜しない
- □ **rather** 副 ①むしろ ②いくぶん, や
  や rather than 〜よりむしろ
- □ **reach for** 〜に手を伸ばす
- □ **reach up** 背伸びをする
- □ **read** 動 ①読む ②〜と書いてある
  read out 声を出して読む
- □ **reader** 名 読者
- □ **readily** 副 すぐに
- □ **ready** 熟 get ready 用意［支度］を
  する ready to 今にも〜しようとし
  ている
- □ **regular** 形 普通の, 標準の
- □ **relation** 名 親戚
- □ **remind** 動 思い出させる
- □ **remove** 動 取り除く
- □ **repeat** 動 繰り返す
- □ **reply** 動 答える
- □ **reqid** 形 required（必須の）のつづ
  り間違い
- □ **reqird** 形 required（必須の）のつづ
  り間違い
- □ **rescue** 動 救う 名 救助, 救出
- □ **reward** 名 報奨金

160

WORD LIST

- **riddle** 名 なぞなぞ
- **right** 熟 all right 大丈夫で, よろしい, 申し分ない, わかった, 承知した
- **ring** 動 (ベルなどを)鳴らす
- **rnser** 名《an－》answer (応答) のつづり間違い
- **rnsr** 名《an－》answer (応答) のつづり間違い
- **roar** 動 ほえる
- **roll** 動 転がる roll down 転がり落ちる
- **Roo** 名 ルー《名前》
- **Roo-noise** 名 ルーの声[立てる音]
- **round** 熟 all round 全体的に, 当たり一面に, 四方に turn round 振り返る
- **rub** 動 こする rub out こすって消す
- **ruler** 名 定規
- **rum-tum-tiddle-um-tum** 間 ラン・タン・ティドル・アン・タン《ハミング》
- **run after** ～を追いかける
- **run away** 走り去る, 逃げ出す
- **run off** 走り去る, 逃げ去る

S

- **sadly** 副 悲しそうに
- **sadness** 名 悲しみ
- **sail off** 出航する
- **sand** 名 砂
- **Sanders** 名 サンダース《名前》
- **satisfy** 動 満足させる, 納得させる
- **say** 動 言う 間 ねえ, 教えて I say あのね say to oneself ひとり言を言う, 心に思う
- **scold** 動 叱る, 小言を言う
- **scratch** 動 ひっかく, こする
- **seagull** 名 カモメ

- **search** 動 捜し求める, 調べる
- **see** 熟 let me see ええと see if ～かどうかを確かめる you see あのね, いいですか
- **seem** 動 (～に)見える, (～のように)思われる seem to be ～であるように思われる
- **sentence** 名 文
- **serious** 形 ①まじめな ②深刻な
- **seriously** 副 真剣に, まじめに
- **settle** 動 解決する, まとまる
- **severely** 副 厳しく
- **shake** 動 振る
- **Shall I ～?** (私が)～しましょうか。
- **shape** 名 形, 姿
- **sharpen** 動 鋭くする, とぐ
- **sheep** 名 羊
- **shelf** 名 棚 top shelf 一番上の棚
- **shine** 動 輝く
- **shook** 動 shake (振る)の過去
- **short** 熟 for short 略して
- **shortness of breath** 息切れ
- **shoulder** 名 肩
- **side** 名 側, 横 from side to side 左右に one side 片側
- **sigh** 動 ため息をつく 名 ため息
- **silence** 名 沈黙, 静寂
- **silent** 形 無言の
- **silently** 副 黙って
- **silly** 形 ばかな, たわいもない
- **simply** 副 単に
- **sinking feeling** 虚脱感, 気がめいる感じ
- **sit on** ～の上に乗る, ～の上に座る
- **slip out** ずり落ちる
- **slope** 名 坂, 斜面
- **slowly** 副 遅く, ゆっくり
- **smash** 名 粉砕(音)

- □ **snack** 名 軽食, おやつ
- □ **sneeze** 動 くしゃみをする
- □ **sniff** 動 鼻をする
- □ **so** 熟 and so そこで, それだから, それで so far ある程度 so that それで, 〜できるように so 〜 that 非常に〜なので…
- □ **soap** 名 石けん
- □ **some** 熟 for quite some time かなり長い間 for some time しばらくの間 for some time now かなり前から
- □ **somebody** 代 誰か, ある人
- □ **someone** 代 ある人, 誰か
- □ **something** 代 ①ある物, 何か ②いくぶん, 多少 something to do 何か〜すべきこと, 何か〜するもの
- □ **sometime** 副 いつか, そのうち
- □ **sometimes** 副 時々, 時たま
- □ **song-and-dance** 名 歌と踊り, 大騒ぎ
- □ **soon** 熟 as soon as 〜するとすぐ, 〜するや否や
- □ **sort** 名 種類, 品質 a sort of 〜のようなもの, 一種の〜 what sort of どういう
- □ **sound like** 〜のように聞こえる
- □ **speak to** 〜と話す
- □ **spell** 動 (語を)つづる, つづりを言う
- □ **spelling** 名 つづり(方)
- □ **spelt** 動 spell (つづる)の過去, 過去分詞
- □ **spill** 動 あふれる
- □ **splash** 名 ざぶん(という音)
- □ **squeak** 動 (動物などが)キュウキュウと鳴く 名 キューキューという鳴き声
- □ **squeaky** 形 キーキーいう
- □ **stair** 名 《-s》階段, 段
- □ **stand up** 立ち上がる

- □ **stare** 動 じっと見る
- □ **start doing** 〜し始める
- □ **start to do** 〜し始める
- □ **stay in** (場所)にとどまる
- □ **stay up** 上げられたままである
- □ **steal** 動 こっそりと手に入れる
- □ **sternly** 副 厳しく
- □ **stick** 名 棒 動 〜を立ち往生させる, 動けなくさせる, 動かない be stuck 行き詰まる, 身動きが取れない
- □ **stiff** 形 こわばった, 堅い
- □ **stiffness** 名 堅いこと, 凝り
- □ **stone** 名 石
- □ **stop doing** 〜するのをやめる
- □ **stoutness** 名 肥満, でっぷりしていること
- □ **stream** 名 小川, 水路
- □ **stretch up** 体を伸ばす
- □ **string** 名 ひも, 糸
- □ **struggle** 動 もがく, 奮闘する
- □ **stuck** 動 stick (動かない)の過去, 過去分詞
- □ **stump** 動 とぼとぼ歩く stump off とぼとぼ立ち去る
- □ **sudden** 形 突然の, 急な
- □ **suit** 名 スーツ, 背広
- □ **sunset** 名 夕焼け
- □ **supper** 名 夕食
- □ **suppose** 動 〜だと想定する, 〜と思う[推定する]
- □ **sure** 熟 make sure 確かめる, 確認する
- □ **surprised** 形 驚いた
- □ **surround** 動 囲む, 包囲する
- □ **suspect** 動 疑わしく思う
- □ **suspicious** 形 疑い深い
- □ **suspiciously** 副 疑い深く
- □ **sustaining** 形 (元気や努力などを)持続させる

WORD LIST

T

- **tail** 名 尾, しっぽ
- **tail-finder** 名 尻尾を見つけた人
- **take** 熟 take a look at ~をちょっと見る take a walk 散歩をする take down 下げる, 降ろす take off ~を取り去る take out 取り出す take someone home ~を家に持ち帰る take ~ out of ~を…から出す take ~ to ~を…に持って行く
- **talk of** ~のことを話す
- **taste** 動 味わう
- **tell** 熟 can never tell with ~のことは分からない tell ~ to ~に…するように言う to tell you the truth 実は, 実を言うと
- **temporary** 形 一時的な
- **than** 熟 rather than ~よりむしろ
- **thank-you** 名 ありがとう(の言葉)
- **that** 熟 after that その後 this and that あれやこれや
- **thaw** 名 雪解け
- **ther** 冠 ザー《クリストファー・ロビン独自の文法による冠詞》
- **there** 熟 down there 下の方で over there あそこに There! ほら! there it is そんな次第だ there you are ①そこにいたのか ②その通りだ there you go ほらね up there あそこで
- **therefore** 副 したがって, その結果
- **thin** 形 やせた get thin やせる
- **thing** 熟 how's things? ごきげんいかが。
- **think of** ~のことを考える, ~を思いつく, 考え出す
- **think to oneself** 心に思う
- **this and that** あれやこれや
- **thistle** 名 アザミ《植物》
- **though** 接 ~だが
- **thoughtful** 形 思慮深い, 考え込んだ

- **thoughtfully** 副 考え込んだ様子で
- **throat** 名 のど
- **throw** 動 投げる throw away ~を捨てる throw ~ down ~を投げ下ろす
- **thrown** 動 throw (投げる)の過去分詞
- **thuthda** 名 birthday (誕生日)のつづり間違い
- **tiddle-iddle** 間 ティドル・イドゥル《ハミング》
- **tight** 形 きつい, 狭い 副 堅く, しっかりと hold on tight to ~をしっかりつかむ
- **tightly** 副 しっかり, 堅く
- **time** 熟 at this time of year 毎年この時期は by this time もうすでに every time ~するときはいつも for quite some time かなり長い間 for some time しばらくの間 for some time now かなり前から for the first time in one's life 生まれて初めて once upon a time むかしむかし
- **tip** 名 先端, 頂点
- **tired** 形 ①疲れた ②あきた, うんざりした
- **tiring** 形 うんざりするような, 退屈な
- **to** 熟 up to ~まで, ~に至るまで
- **toe** 名 つま先
- **tole** 動 told (伝えた)《pole と韻を踏むために語末の d を落としている》
- **tongue** 名 舌
- **too much** 過度の
- **too ~ to** …するには~すぎる
- **top** 熟 on top of ~の上(部)に top shelf 一番上の棚
- **towel** 名 タオル
- **towel-rack** 名 タオルかけ

163

WINNIE-THE-POOH

- [ ] **track** 名通った跡 動追跡する
- [ ] **tra-la-la** 間タラ・ラ・ラ《ハミング》
- [ ] **trap** 名わな
- [ ] **trappy** 形罠っぽい
- [ ] **tree-root** 名木の根
- [ ] **trespasser** 名侵入者
- [ ] **Trespassers William** トレスパッサーズ・ウィリアム《Trespassers will be prosecuted（侵入者は起訴されます）の看板がwillの後ろで折れて名前だと勘違いされている》
- [ ] **trick** 動だます
- [ ] **trip** 動つまづく，転ぶ
- [ ] **truth** 名真実 **to tell you the truth** 実は，実を言うと
- [ ] **try hard to** ～に尽力する
- [ ] **turn into** ～に変わる
- [ ] **turn round** 振り返る
- [ ] **turn to** ～の方を向く
- [ ] **tut-tut** 間ちぇっ《舌打ち》
- [ ] **twinkle** 動きらきら光る，輝く
- [ ] **two** 熟**a ～ or two** 1～か2～，2，3の

U

- [ ] **umty-tiddly, umty-too** 間アムティ・ティドゥリィ・アムティ・トゥー《ハミング》
- [ ] **unable** 形《be–to》～することができない
- [ ] **unfavorable** 形不都合な，好ましくない
- [ ] **unknown** 形未知の
- [ ] **unless** 接もし～でなければ
- [ ] **unlucky** 形不運な
- [ ] **up and down** 行ったり来たり，あちこちと
- [ ] **up there** あそこで
- [ ] **up to** ～まで，～に至るまで

- [ ] **upon** 前《日・時》～に **once upon a time** むかしむかし
- [ ] **usual** 形通常の，普通の

V

- [ ] **verse** 名詩の1行，節
- [ ] **very well** 結構，よろしい

W

- [ ] **wake up** 起きる，目を覚ます
- [ ] **walk** 熟**go for a walk** 散歩に行く **take a walk** 散歩をする **walk along**（前へ）歩く **walk around** 歩き回る，ぶらぶら歩く **walk away** 立ち去る，遠ざかる **walk on** 歩き続ける
- [ ] **wander up and down** 行ったり来たりする
- [ ] **waterfall** 名滝
- [ ] **wave** 動①揺らす ②（手などを振って）合図する
- [ ] **way** 熟**all the way down** 端から端まで **all the way to** ～までずっと **find one's way** たどり着く **push one's way through** かき分けて進む **way to** ①～する方法 ②～に行く道
- [ ] **well** 熟**very well** 結構，よろしい
- [ ] **wet** 動ぬれる
- [ ] **what** 熟**What about ～?** ～についてあなたはどう思いますか。～はどうですか。 **What's the matter?** どうしたんですか。 **what if** もし～だったらどうなるだろうか **what sort of** どういう
- [ ] **whatever** 代どんなこと[もの]が～とも
- [ ] **whatever-it-is** 代それが何であっても
- [ ] **whatever-it-was** 代それが何であったとしても

164

WORD LIST

- [ ] **whenever** 接 ～するたびに
- [ ] **wherefore** 副 どういう理由で
- [ ] **whether** 接 ～かどうか
- [ ] **which** 圏 **In which** The chapter ［story］in which ～の略
- [ ] **while** 熟 **after a while** しばらくして **for a while** しばらくの間, 少しの間
- [ ] **whisker** 名《-s》ほおひげ
- [ ] **whisper** 動 ささやく, 小声で話す 名 ささやき
- [ ] **whistle** 動 口笛を吹く
- [ ] **who** 熟 **anybody who** ～する人はだれでも
- [ ] **whole** 形 全体の, すべての
- [ ] **Why not?** どうしてだめなのですか。
- [ ] **wide** 形 幅の広い
- [ ] **Will you ～?** ～してくれませんか。
- [ ] **wink** 動 ウインクする
- [ ] **Winnie-the-Pooh** 名 ウィニー・ザ・プー《名前》
- [ ] **wipe** 動 ～をふく, ぬぐう
- [ ] **wisdom** 名 知恵
- [ ] **wise** 形 聡明な, 博学の
- [ ] **wish** 熟 **I wish ～ were here** ～がここにいればいいのになあ。《仮定法過去》
- [ ] **Wizzle** 名 ウィズル《イタチに似た架空の動物》
- [ ] **wobble** 動 ふらつく, ぐらぐらする
- [ ] **wobbly** 形 定まらない, ぐらつく
- [ ] **woke** 動 wake（目が覚める）の過去
- [ ] **wonder** 動 不思議に思う,（～かしらと）思う **wonder about** ～について知りたがる **wonder if** ～ではないかと思う
- [ ] **Woozle** 名 ウーズル《イタチに似た架空の動物》
- [ ] **world** 熟 **in the world** 世界で

- [ ] **worse** 形 いっそう悪い
- [ ] **Would you like ～?** ～はいかがですか。
- [ ] **Would you ～?** ～してくださいませんか。
- [ ] **would like to** ～したいと思う
- [ ] **write down** 書き留める
- [ ] **write out** 書き上げる

Y

- [ ] **year** 熟 **for years and years** 長年
- [ ] **yet** 熟 **not yet** まだです
- [ ] **you see** あのね, いいですか

English Conversational Ability Test
国際英語会話能力検定

● E-CATとは…
英語が話せるようになるためのテストです。インターネットベースで、30分であなたの発話力をチェックします。

www.ecatexam.com

● iTEP®とは…
世界各国の企業、政府機関、アメリカの大学300校以上が、英語能力判定テストとして採用。オンラインによる90分のテストで文法、リーディング、リスニング、ライティング、スピーキングの5技能をスコア化。iTEP®は、留学、就職、海外赴任などに必要な、世界に通用する英語力を総合的に評価する画期的なテストです。

www.itepexamjapan.com

ラダーシリーズ
Winnie-the-Pooh くまのプーさん [新版]

2019年6月9日　第1刷発行
2024年7月11日　第4刷発行

原著者　A. A. ミルン

発行者　賀川　洋

発行所　IBCパブリッシング株式会社
　　　　〒162-0804 東京都新宿区中里町29番3号
　　　　菱秀神楽坂ビル
　　　　Tel. 03-3513-4511　Fax. 03-3513-4512
　　　　www.ibcpub.co.jp

© IBC Publishing, Inc. 2019

印刷　株式会社シナノパブリッシングプレス
装丁　伊藤　理恵　　イラスト　E. H. シェパード
組版データ　Sabon Roman + Akko Rounded Std Regular

落丁本・乱丁本は、小社宛にお送りください。送料小社負担にてお取り替えいたします。本書の無断複写（コピー）は著作権法上での例外を除き禁じられています。

Printed in Japan
ISBN978-4-7946-0581-8

IBC対訳ライブラリー

英語で読む
クマのプーさん
[新版]

本書の英文に日本語訳と
音声ダウンロードが付いた
人気のシリーズです！

音声
ダウンロード
付き

ポイント1 初級者から楽しめます！

本書の英文とイラストそのまま*に、ページごとに和訳がついています。
各ページの下欄に、重要語句・表現の意味を載せています。**
(*ページレイアウトは本書とは異なります。**巻末に辞書はありません。)

ポイント2 文法や英語表現が学べます！

本文の英文から役立つ英語表現をピックアップし、
多数の例文とともに詳しく解説しています。

ポイント3 朗読音声が付いています！

本文中のQRコードをお手持ちのスマホで読み取って、音声を聞く
ことができます。

> クマのプーさんの
> かわいらしい言い間違えや、
> クリストファー・ロビンの
> スペルミスも、わかりやすく
> 翻訳されています。

イクラス・アブドゥル・ハディ 英文リライト
牛原眞弓 日本語訳
船田秀佳 英語解説

A5判　256ページ　本体価格 1900円
ISBN 978-4-7946-0778-2